HIGHER EDUCATION IN INDIA
Development and Problems

B. DEKA

ATLANTIC
PUBLISHERS & DISTRIBUTORS (P) LTD

Published by

ATLANTIC

PUBLISHERS & DISTRIBUTORS (P) LTD

7/22, Ansari Road, Darya Ganj,
New Delhi-110002
Phones : +91-11-40775252, 23273880, 23275880, 23280451
Fax : +91-11-23285873
Web : www.atlanticbooks.com
E-mail : orders@atlanticbooks.com

Branch Office
5, Nallathambi Street, Wallajah Road,
Chennai-600002
Phones : +91-44-64611085, 32413319
E-mail : chennai@atlanticbooks.com

Printed in India at Glorious Printers, A-13, D.S.I.D.C.,
Jhilmil Industrial Area, Delhi-110095

Preface

This book is the result of my long term investigation. This book has been designed primarily as a book of development and problems of Higher Education of India. There are some books on Higher Education in India but in this book I have attempted to narrate the important topics of Higher Education and its problems in a lucid and analytical manner. I do not claim much that this book is fully original. In the introductory chapter I have discussed the role and objectives of Higher education of India. The book is mainly intended for the teacher students of orientation course. Students of degree classes will also find it helpful and to those who go for higher studies, it may serve as ground work. It is for the reader to judge to what extent the author has succeeded in his efforts. Suggestions, if any, for the improvement of the book from students, teachers and respected readers would be welcomed.

I am very grateful to Prof. C.L. Anand, Ex-Vice Chancellor, Arunachal University, Prof. J. Mahanty, Ex-A.S.C. Director Utkal University, Dr. P. Sarma, Ex-Director of A.S.C., Gauhati University and Staff members of the Department of Education, Calcutta University and my reverent teacher Dr. L. Das for their valuable advice.

I extend my thanks to all the authors and Publishers for consulting and quoting their valuable books. In the preparation of the book I have gone through different kinds of documents, government publications which have been duly listed in the bibliography given at the end. I expresse my gratitude to the writers and Publishers of all these documents/publications.

Lastly, I offer my grateful thanks to the management of Atlantic Publishers and Distributors, New Delhi for the keen interest they have evinced in bringing out this book.

B. DEKA

Contents

In

purpose o

The true

instead o

should

society

as has

from the

the light

and sover

different

Educa

whatever

educatio

character

like laws

differ fro

not depen

There

effective

itself me

things n

to an en

political

theory an

among

in the

Introduction

ROLE OF EDUCATION

In determining the aims and ideals of man's life the purpose of education has to play a vital and significant role. The true education must make the individual free and easy instead of making sophisticated and complex. Thus, the aim should have the quest for a simpler, serene and co-operative society to be accomplished with the vision of a better society as has been defined and discussed, many a time by thinkers from the political, economic and social view point. Education is the light of life which can bring about the concept of self-rule and sovereign democracy in the lives of people. It conveys different meaning for different regions under different spheres.[1]

Education includes whatever we do for ourselves and whatever to be done for us by others. The overt purpose of education is to bring us nearer to the perfection of our nature, character and human faculties. Because these virtuous things like laws, government industrial arts, modes of social life which differ from one another by climate, soil and local position and not dependent on human will.[2]

There can be no doubt that education should play an effective role in all varied circumstances. Because education itself means an endless process of becoming and moulding the things newer and better than before. It is very much sensitive to an environment like industrial area, to the distinct type of political ideology prevailing among different people. Thus, the theory and practice of education may differ substantially even among countries having many affinities. In spite of the multiplicity in the broader dimension of education, local demands and conditions, facts have their impacts on theory and practice of education and that is why it can be said that education practices are not 'importable commodity'.[3]

Moreover, education should usher the finest minds to grapple with the labour of thought to thrash out the difficult problems of science, sociology, economics, politics and ethics which beset the path of man. The primary function of education is to question and probe and doubt not to take things for granted. So the quest with education is more important than the truth.

Education has to be a socially integrated institution that forms the part of human civilization. Real education is primarily a process of training of the hand, heart and head, in the art of thing a happy and co-operate life. Thus, the purpose of education may be summed up as three-fold, *viz.*,

(1) acquisition of a certain amount of knowledge,

(2) requisition of culture,

(3) attaining the capability to get a suitable profession.

ROLE OF HIGHER EDUCATION IN OUR NATIONAL LIFE

Higher education plays an important role in developing the nation to a great extent. It helps the members of the society to get lives, to develop well and to improve the strength of the nation. It inculcates to reform conduct and behaviours and integrity of personality in the individuals. There is pursuit of truth and excellence in man and only the higher education can direct the right path of it. On the whole since the past higher education has been playing its due role in developing the nation to a greater extent though not to the extent desired.

Higher education reforms our society from different points of view. The high class cultured people come out from the institutions of higher education. Colleges are the principal centres of higher education. But Universities being the ultimate controller of them, are more responsible to it. Because it manages the rules and regulations of the colleges. These institutions are the controller of Degree examining and affiliating authorities for the venture colleges that can fulfil the conditions required including the territorial limits. It does not directly manage the colleges but it lays down conditions to which they must conform in order to obtain and retain affiliation, and if satisfied itself as to the absence of the conditions by inspection.[4]

Universities are the seats of higher learning from where the society gets its leaders of national life. The aim and purpose of higher education is to provide an integrated and coherent picture of creation. University is a home of learning and it is upon the standard and efficiency of teaching and the degree of capacity of these seats of higher knowledge that the standard and efficiency of the mental and moral acquisitions of the society depends. 'If India is to confront the confusion of our times, she must turn for guidance, not of those who are lost in the exigencies of the passion hour, but to her men of science, to her poets and artists, to her discoverers and inventors. These intellectual pioneers of civilisation are to be found and trained in the universities, which are the sanctuaries of the inner life of the nation.'[5]

The prosperity of the country is linked up with the University. A vicious university is like a contaminated fountain which is bound to imperil the health of those who drink from it. The fate of a nation is shaped and moulded in the University.[6]

The role of University in developing democratic country like India which has set before itself the task of establishing socio-economic justice, is of a very significant and revolutionary. Broadly stating, the purpose of University education in India today must be to educate men and women who will promote the development of society to the highest attainable level.

In discharging their functions, our Universities have also to take care to guard the Indian society against the danger of ignoring the pre-eminent place of culture in the healthy development of the nation. In the pursuits of its socio-economic policies, the nation is sometimes apt to concentrate the economic problems and is likely to forget the significance of cultural pre-requisites of a democratic way of life. Undoubtedly it is the primary function of the University to promote and transmit knowledge in all its branches and to help to create a vigorous and progressive class of experts and technicians in the several branches of knowledge. But while pursuing the important function, the Universities must also incessantly try to discharge their functions of promoting and transmitting the essential features of culture.[7]

OBJECTIVES OF HIGHER EDUCATION

The objectives of higher education are to promote welfare of individuals as to strengthen the nation. It is to inculcate high standards of conduct and behaviour and integrety of personality in the individual members. There is pursuit of truth and excellence in all its diversity, a pursuit which needs, above all, courage and fearlessness.

The Education Commission of 1964-66 enumerated many objectives of higher education. They are :

1. to seek and cultivate new knowledge, to engage vigorously and fearlessly in the pursuit of truth and to interpret old knowledge and beliefs in the light of new needs and discoveries,
2. to provide the right kind of leadership in all walks of life, to identify gifted youth and help them develop their potential to the full by cultivating physical fitness, developing the powers of the mind and cultivating right interests, attitudes and moral and intellectual values,
3. to provide society with competent men and women, trained in agriculture, arts, medicine, science and technology and various other professions, who will also be cultivated individuals, imbued with a sense of social purpose,
4. to strive to promote equality and social and cultural

differences through diffusion of education and

5. to foster in the teachers and students, and through them in a society generally, the attitudes and values needed for developing the 'good life' in individuals and society.[8]

Again the Commission expressed the view as :

'The Principal object is to deepen man's understanding of the Universe and of himself in body, mind and spirit and to disseminate this understanding throughout society and to apply it in the service of mankind.'

Pandit Jawaharlal Nehru expressed his view as :

'A university stands for humanism, for tolerance, for reason, for adventure of ideas and for the search of truth. It stands for the onward march of the human race towards even higher objectives. If the Universities discharge their duties adequately, then it is well with the nation and the people.'[9]

HIGHER EDUCATION IN INDIA (HISTORICAL BACKGROUND)

Higher education in India has a long history of its own and has a long tradition in learning. In the past, higher education played an important role. Corresponding to the colleges of modern times, there were 'Gurukulas' and 'ashrams' run by individual scholars in ancient times. The curriculum in these single teacher's institutions were fairly wide and embraced all fields of intellectual activities including such subjects as archery and principles of warfare. There also existed many parishads or assemblies of renowned scholars where disputable points in connection with religion were discussed. Individual students also approached these institutions for the recognition of their merits. The earliest university was 'Takshashilla' which attained great fame as a university by seventh century B.C.[10]

Education was regarded as the most important tool for self realisation in ancient time. During ancient period there were two significant impacts on education. The first of these was the impact of the Aryan civilization and the second was the Buddhistic influence. During the beginning of the Aryan period, the education imported, was generally confined to the priestly class, and later it spread to the two other classes. The 'kshatriyas' and the 'Vaishas'.[11] During the Buddhist and Jain period, education took on a different character. One main difference between Aryan and Buddhist education was that the latter was not based on Vedic study and its teachers were not of priestly class. It was open to all irrespective of caste, creed and sex. Buddhist education and learning, centred round in monasteries. The Buddhist world did not offer any educational opportunities. All education, sacred as well as secular, were in the hands of monks. Some of the monasteries developed into a kind of educational centres. The University of Purushapura (Peswar), Takshashila, (West Punjab), Jagaddal (Bihar), Jayender Vihara (Kashmir), Kanchi (Madras), Vallabhi (Saurastra) and other centres were some of the famous places. These institutions were richly endowed, they attracted students from far and near, especially Nalanda and Taxila had acquired an international reputation. The studies too were fairly comprehensive and included ritual and holy scriptures, grammar and astronomy, medicine, logic and the different systems of Philosophy.[12]

> The Chinese traveller, Hieun Tsang wrote about Nalanda : 'The priests to the number of several thousands, are men of the highest ability and talent. Their distinction is very great at the present time, and there are many hundred whose fame has rapidly spread through distant regions. From morning till night, they engage in discussion. The old and the young mutually help one another.'[13]

During Muslim period most of the Universities of Buddhist period had disappeared. A few Tols and Pathsalas (Hindu advanced learning) were existed in the beginning of the nineteenth century A.D. The Muslims also established their own institutions of Higher education which were known as Madrasahs. The institutions had existed in the cities like Delhi, Lucknow, Agra, Jaipur, Azmir, Murshidabad and in some other places. The curriculum of these institutions included grammar, rhetoric, logic, Law, History, Philosophy, Geometry and Astronomy. The medium of instruction generally was Persian, but study of Arabic was compulsory for Muslim students.[14] Under the Tuglok dynasty, Muslim education seems to have made considerable progress. The Muhammedian historian 'Ferishta' says that Feroze built not less than 30 colleges with mosques attached. On the other hand, during the period of Akbar, education made great progress. The monarch was deeply interested in the work of spreading education and learning. During his period residential colleges were made in various branches of learning like Mathematics, Geometry, Astronomy, Physics, Philosophy, History, Grammar, Literature, etc.[15]

When British occupied the country, higher education was more or less dislocated. A number of English and Oriental Colleges, Government and private, were established in 1857. These institutions were quite different from the colleges of today. The Majority of them grew out of schools, teaching English and conducted classes 'in which the alphabet was taught under the same roof with classes reading Shakespear, the calculus, Smith's 'Wealth of Nation' and 'the Ramayana'.[16]

Modern type of higher education began during the British rule, Higher educational institutions were established in the imitation of London University after the recommendations of wood's Despatch of 1854. Bombay, Calcutta and Madras were the earliest of these Universities, all were founded in 1857 and the University of Punjab and Allahabd were incorporated in the lines of the old Universities in 1882 and 1887. They all began as purely a non-residential and examining bodies and contained to be so till the opening of the present century, when the Indian University Act was passed in 1904. By 1901-1902 there was a rapid expansion of college education. As against 68 colleges in 1881-82 there were 179 affiliated colleges in 1901-1902.[17]

Indian University Commission of 1902 was appointed during

Lord Curzons Viceroyality. It was a landmark in the University Education. It was directed "to enquire into the condition and prospects of the Universities established in British India." As Lord Curzon observed "How different in India : here the University has no corporate existence in the same sense (as in Oxford and Cambridge) of the term, it is not a collection of buildings, it is sincerely even a site. It is a body that controls courses of study and sets examination' papers to the pupils of affiliated colleges. They are not part of it. They are frequently not in the same city, sometimes men in the same province."[18] Indian University Commission 1902 studied the conditions of higher education and made certain recommendations and brought about some desirable changes by which the functions of the Universities were extended. But the Commission rejected the idea of establishing new Universities at Aligarh, Benaras, Patna, Dacca, Rangoon and Nagpur. The purpose of the Indian University Commission was formulated as follows :

> "To enquire into the conditions and prospects of the Universities established in India to consider and report upon any proposals which have been or may be made for improving their constitution and working and to recommend to the Governor General in Council such measures as may tend to elevate the standard of University teaching and to promote the advancement of learning."[19]

On March 11, 1904 Lord Curzon published his educational policy in the form of a Government resolution. As regard the quality of education his view was, that the higher education is pursuit with too exclusive a view to entering government service; that its scope is thus unduly narrowed and that those who fail to obtain employment under the government, are ill fitted for other pursuits.[20]

As a result of Curzon's educational policy the number of colleges were gradually increased and workload of the University became heavier. It was the government of Lord Hardings who surveyed the situation and issued a resolution in 1913. It accepted the need for establishing more Universities. It said,

"It is necessary to restrict the area over which the affiliating Universities have control by securing in the first instance, a separate University for each of the leading provinces in India and secondly creates new local teaching and residential University within each of the provinces in harmony with the best modern opinion as to the right road to educational efficiency." In response to the policy five new universities like Benaras and Mysore in 1916, Patna in 1917, Hyderabad in 1918, S.N.D.T. Women University in 1916 comes into existence.[21]

In the year of 1917 the Calcutta University Commission was appointed to investigate the problems of higher Education. It made certain recommendations as a result of which a number of new Universities sprang up. After 1921 when education was transferred into Indian control, the development of Universities was much faster and during the next 26 years fourteen more Universities were established. These were Lucknow in 1921, Nagpur in 1923, Daca and Rangoon in 1920, Aligarh in 1921, Delhi in 1922, Andhra in 1926, Agra in 1927, Annamalai in 1929, Tribancore in 1937, Utkal in 1943, Saugar in 1946, Sindh and Rajputana in 1947.[22] With the rapid increases of Universities the number of affiliated colleges as well as enrollment were increased.

TABLE 1

The table shows the Growth and Development of Universities in India before Independence.[23]

Name of University	Years of Establishment
Calcutta University	1857
Bombay University	1857
Madras University	1857
Panjab University	1882
Allahabad University	1887
Banaras University	1916
Mysore University	1916
S.N.D.T. Women University	1916
Patna University	1917

Name of University	Years of Establishment
Hyderabad University	1918
Lucknow University	1921
Nagpur University	1923
Rangoon University	1923
Dacca University	1921
Aligarh University	1921
Delhi University	1922
Andhra University	1926
Agra University	1927
Annamalai University	1929
Trivancore University	1937
Utkal University	1943
Saugarh University	1946
Sindh University	1947
Rajputana University	1947

Source : Mukherjee, S.N., Acharya Book Depot, Vadoddara, 1976, p. 173.

EDUCATION AFTER INDEPENDENCE

India got her Independence in the year of 1947. The colour of higher education changed and became brighter day by day. As a result, institutions for higher education were established by the public and the government. In the post-Independence era, the expansion of higher education was rapid and unique.

It was deemed proper that a preliminary survey should be made of the financial and teaching conditions in the Universities prior to framing and plans for the improvement and expansions of Indian University education. Hence, the Inter University Board and Central Advisory Board of Education had passed a resolution recommending to the Indian Government to appoint a commission in consultation with the State Government "to report on Indian University Education and suggest improvement and extension that may be desirable to suit present and future requirements of the country. The government accepted this resolution and in November, 1948, a University Education Commission was appointed under the chairmanship of Dr. S. Radhakrishnan."[24]

The Commission submitted the first part of the Report in eighteen chapters covering seven hundred and forty seven pages. It has taken all the main problems pertaining to University education into account. The second part of it contains figures, statistics and evidence etc. In the beginning, making brief historical retrospect of University education in India, the Commission has placed the aims of University education in the new political and social structure of the country.

The Commission suggests the following points :

(1) Problem of teachers, (2) Standard of teaching, (3) Curriculum, (4) Post-Graduate Training and Research, (5) Professional education, (6) Religious Education, (7) Medium of instruction, (8) The system of examination, (9) Students, their activities and Welfare, (10) Women education etc.

A special meeting of the Central Advisory Board of Education was held on 22nd and 23rd April, 1950 in order to discuss the recommendations of the Commission making necessary amendments their in. Recommendations with regard to Post-Graduate education and research were accepted and those dealing with professional education, specially, Agriculture, Commerce, Education, Engineering, Technology, Law and Medical Science were accepted only with certain amendments. Besides, recommendations with regard to the medium of instruction, classification of Teachers, their salaries and conditions of service, curriculum, objective evaluation of examination, women's education, incorporation of fresh universities and student's welfare activities were also accepted readily by the Board.[25]

Thus, in accordance with the recommendations of the University Commission, a University Grants Commission was established in November, 1953 by a resolution of the Ministry of Education for the purpose of allocation and disbursement of grants to universalities as well as for the purpose of co-ordination and maintenance of standards of education in India. The power and functions of the Commission were enlarged in January, 1954. The constituent colleges of the University of Delhi were brought within the purview of the Commission in April, 1955. The Commission has since 1956 under the University Grants Commission Act, 1956 as passed by the Parliament with effect from this date the Commission has been reconstituted with a chairman and eight members.[26]

Again government of India appointed another commission to enquire the condition and problems of Secondary Education of India. In the words of the Secondary Education Commission Report (1952-53) "The Universities dominated secondary schools in every respect. Secondary education, instead of being a self-sufficient course preparing students to enter life after completing the course, because merely a step towards the Universities and University colleges, with the result that schools could not function with an independent programme of their own."[27]

The report of Education Commission of 1964 is known as National Education Commission or Kothari commission. It defined the development of Higher education as "It is obvious that if higher education is not radically improved, our administration and technical progress, our intellectual standards and social advance, will all be most seriously handicapped.''[28] Improvement in the system of Higher education and its development to serve the Indian society are deemed to be imperative needs. The Education Commission made numerous recommendations for the development and improvement. Some important recommendations are given below :

(1) establishment of six major universities, where first class post-graduate work and research could be possible,

(2) establishment of clusters of advanced centres in the major universities, at least 50 in the next 5 or 10 years to promote inter-disciplinary research,

(3) improvement of other universities and affiliated colleges, providing teachers of quality and helping them through concentration or resources to raise them to the level of centre of advance studies,

(4) development of affiliated colleges by granting autonomous status to outstanding colleges,

(5) improvement of teaching and evaluation by encouraging independent study under the guidance of instructors, discouraging of memorising, development of individual contacts with teachers,

(6) improvement of quality and content of lecturing and introducing a system of internal and continuous evaluation to replace the external examination in all teaching Universities, continuation of both — internal and external evaluation in other places,

(7) Universities should evolve dynamic technique of management and organization suited to their special functions and purposes in order to have improved governance and so on.[29]

The Education Commission has also made recommendations on the appointment of Vice-Chancellors. Inter University collaboration, development of advanced educational research, autonomy with the university, students services, unions and discipline, medium of education, expansion of higher education, part time higher education, size of the colleges, reorganization of courses etc.

As regards the structure of higher education, the Commission has visualised "a higher education stage having a course of three years or more for the first degree and followed by courses for the second or research degrees varying durations."[30]

As against and enrollment of 20,65,041 students in 86 Universities, nine institutions deemed to be Universities and 3,896 colleges in the year 1971-72 there were 29,52,006 students enrolled in 1981-82 in as many as 118 Universities, 13 institutions deemed to be Universities and 4,886 colleges and today we have 193+34 Universities and 8,197 colleges and enrollment of 49,97,000.

Growth in the number of institutions and enrollment for the period 1951-61 to 1997-98, is shown in the table 2(A). Figures pertaining to students enrollment in Intermediate, Pre-University and professional classes.

TABLE 2(A)

Table shows the Growth and Development of Universities and Colleges with Students' Enrollment from 1951-1998

Year	Number of Universities		Number of Colleges	Students' Enrollment
1951-61	22		695	N.A.
1971-72	86+9	(Deemed to be Universities)	3896	20,65,041
1972-73	90+9	(-do-)	4158	21,68,107
1973-74	95+9	(-do-)	4170	22,34,385
1974-75	102+9	(-do-)	4170	23,66,541
1975-76	102+9	(-do-)	4272	24,26,109
1976-77	105+9	(-do-)	4317	24,31,563
1977-78	108+9	(-do-)	4375	25,64,972
1978-79	108+10	(-do-)	4460	26,18,228
1979-80	108+11	(-do-)	4558	25,48,579
1980-81	112+11	(-do-)	4722	27,52,437
1981-82	118+13	(-do-)	4886	29,52,006
1985-86	127+18	(-do-)	5500	N.A.
1988-89	144+25	(-do-)	6779	40,74,676
1989-90	146+28	(-do-)	6942	42,46,878
1990-91	147+29	(-do-)	7121	44,25,247
1993-94	172+28	(-do-)	7600	46,20,000
1994-95	187+34	(-do-)	8000	48,50,000
1997-98	193+34	(-do-)	8197	49,97,000

N.A. Not Available

Source : (1) University Grants Commission Report, 1981-82, 1988-89, 1990-91.

(2) University News April II, 1994, June 6, 1994, p. 2.

(3) University News, Sept., 1998.

TABLE 2(B)

Table shows the Growth of Students' Enrollment in Higher Educational Institution in India from 1969-70 to 1997-1998

Year	Total Enrollment	Increase over the Preceding Year	Percentage of Increase
1969-70	17,92,780	2,26,677	14.5
1970-71	19,53,700	1,60,920	9.0
1971-72	20,65,041	1,11,341	5.7
1972-73	21,68,107	1,03,066	5.0
1973-74	22,34,385	66,278	3.1
1974-75	23,66,541	1,32,156	5.9
1975-76	24,26,109	59,568	2.5
1976-77	24,31,563	5,454	0.2
1977-78	25,64,972	1,33,400	5.5
1978-79	26,18,228	53,256	2.1
1979-80	26,48,579	30,351	1.2
1980-81	27,52,437	1,03,858	3.9
1981-82	29,52,066	1,90,629	7.3
1982-83	31,33,093	1,81,027	6.1
1983-84	33,07,649	1,74,556	5.6
1984-85	34,04,096	96,447	2.9
1985-86	35,70,897	1,66,801	4.9
1986-87	36,81,870	1,10,973	3.1
1987-88	38,14,417	1,32,547	3.6
1988-89	39,47,922	1,33,505	3.5
1989-90	42,46,878	1,72,202	4.1
1990-91	44,25,247	1,76,369	4.2
1993-94	46,20,000	NA	NA
1997-98	49,97,000	NA	NA

N.A. : Not Available

Sources : 1. University Grants Commission Report for the year 1988-89, p. iv (App. II).

2. UGC Report 1990-91.

3. University News, April II, 1994.

4. University News, Sept., 1998.

NOTES

1. Mukerjee, S.N., *Education in India To-day and Tomorrow* 1976, p. 168, Acharya Book Depot. Vadodara.
2. Faure Edgar and Others, *Learning to be*, Sterling Publishers, Delhi, 1973, p. xv.
3. Agarwal and Singh, *All India Educational Directory*, Chandigarh, 1972, p. 1(a).
4. Das, K.K., *Current Problems of Indian Education,* Scientific Book Depot, Cuttuk-1, 1971, pp. 76-77.
5. Rawat, P.L., *History of Indian Education*, 1985, Ram Prasad and Sons, Agra, p. 318.
6. *Ibid.,* p. 318.
7. A.I.U. University News, *University Autonomy Its Meaning Today*, Paper 7, International Association of University, p. 5, June, 1986.
8. Kothari, D.S., *Kothari Commission*, NCERT, 1971, p. 497, 1964-66.
9. Kothari, D.S., *Kothari Commission* 1964-66, NCERT, 1971, p. 495.
10. Altaker, A.S., *Education in Ancient India*, Nand Kishore and Bros., Varanasi, 1958, p. 186.
11. *Ibid.*, p. 189
12. Keay, F.E., *A History of Education in India*, Oxford University Press, Delhi, pp. 91-92.
13. Kochar, S.K., *Pivotal Issues in Indian Education*, 1982, p. 2, Sterling Publishers Pvt. Ltd., New Delhi.
14. Keay, F.E., *A History of Education in India*, Oxford University Press, pp. 107-113.
15. *Ibid.,* p. 115.
16. Mukerjee, S.N., *Education in India Today and Tomorrow*, Acharya Book Depot, Vadodara, 1976, p. 166.
17. *Ibid.,* p. 167.
18. Shah, A.B., *Higher Education in India*, Lalvani Publishing House, New Delhi, 1967, p. 10.
19. Rawat, P.L., *History of Indian Education*, Ram Prasads and Sons, Agra 3, 1985, p. 202.
20. *Ibid.,* p. 203.
21. Mukerjee, S.N., *Education in India today and Tomorrow*, Acharya Book Depot, Vadodara, 1978, p. 171.
22. *Ibid.,* p. 169.
23. *Ibid.,* p. 172.

24. Rawat, P.L., *History of Indian Education*, Ramprasad and Sons, Agra, 1985, p. 321.
25. *Ibid.*, p. 329.
26. Kochar, S.K., *Pivotal Issues in Indian Education*, Sterling Publishers Pvt. Ltd., New Delhi, 1982, p. 3.
27. *Ibid.*, p. 9
28. Kothari, D.S., *Kothari Commission* 1964-66, NCERT, 1971, p. 73.
29. *Ibid.*, p. 506.
30. *Ibid.*, p. 74.

1

Technical Education

INTRODUCTION

The greatest challenge for education is to meet the needs of the society. The development of science and technology has occupied the modern age and their wonders are perceptible all round. Science has enabled us to win nature, earth and heaven. The progressive countries have made tremendous progress through the development of science and technology. This has been possible because of the availability of material resources in abundance. They have made maximum utilisation of these resources and are supposed to be the most industrialised countries in the world.

The present day need of Indian society is to increase productivity. It naturally resulted in the inability of our country to compete successfully with other progressive nations of the world in the spheres of industrial development. India too is rich in both material and human resources. What is needed in their proper tapping and utilisation? This requires expansion and development of technical and vocational education.[1]

Technical education has a supreme importance in the modern times. There is some distinction between vocational education, industrial education and technical education. Technical education, in contrast to the other types of education, is that which emphasises on the learning of techniques as technical procedures and necessary skills and aims at preparing technicians usually above the secondary level.[2]

The Government of India Science Policy Resolution in 1953 expressed that 'India's enormous resources of manpower can only become an asset in the modern world when trained and educated. The use of human material for industrialisation demands, its education in science and training in technical and vocational skills."[3]

OBJECTIVES OF TECHNICAL EDUCATION

Objectives of technical education are as follows :

(1) to provide many routes for technical competency;

(2) to secure services of better qualified man to man the industry;

(3) to help expansion of industries;

(4) to generate new ideas and create activities which will lead to the development of industry;

(5) to improve skill in different vocations, trades and crafts;

(6) to enhance occupational chances and thus provide occupational opportunities to a large number of people and solve unemployment;

(7) to meet the demand for well-qualified technical personnel;

(8) to develop good habits of work, co-operation and character;

(9) to enable one to gauge ones own abilities and aptitudes, and help in right placement of right personal in right positions;

(10) to develop honest workmanship, desire for perfection, efficiency and manual dexterity;

(11) to enable one to get the job of self expression and creating something with his own hands, using his brains;

(12) to increase the national productivity and wealth in turn and so on.[4]

According to the draft 6th Plan "The technical education system represents a national resources of science and technology with specialised laboratories sophisticated instrumentation facilities, and more importantly, teams of highly qualified scientific and engineering personnel on their faculty. These internal resources should be utilised not merely towards technological self reliance but also to bring about progressive improvement in the quality of technical education."[5]

HISTORICAL BACKGROUND

Technical education in India has grown under the pressure of necessity along various lines including industrial, engineering and technological training. India was noted for the superior quality of its science and technology in ancient times. Mohen jodero was one of the good examples of our knowledge of town planning, civil engineering and architecture. Even earlier Rigveda spoke about canals and dams. When Alexander, the great invaded this country, among the things he took away, were steel ingots, suggesting an era when India produced steel of fine quality, a blight seemed to have descended in the country.[6]

If we study the present situation of the development of technology of the world, we have seen that our country was decayed that other countries of the world that made progress. For example, U.S.A. was a primitive economy hardly a century back. Today the same country maintains millions with food to such an excess that maize is burnt down, and milk is thrown into streams for maintaining a high price level. The average life of an American is 76 years twice that of Indian.[7] Now more than sixty years ago, even Japan was far behind India both in agriculture and industries. But during these sixty years while India made some progress, Japan built-up her agriculture and manufacturing industries through scientific organisation of her general and technical education. Great changes have taken place in USSR during the last fifty years, seven year plans have changed her from agrarian country into an advanced industrial one.[8]

The latter part of the 18th century was a crucial period of technical education. The education system of this period was influenced by the policy of the East India Company. The company needed some Indian clerks and officials for its various departments in order to manage affairs well. The company stood in need of engineers of constructing roads, canals and government building under the public works department. In 1824 the Native Society of Bombay had opened classes in engineering and mother tongue was used as the medium of instruction. Engineering classes were started at the Elphinstone Institute in the year 1844, and at Pune in 1854. At Madras, education in Engineering could not be inaugurated until the incorporation of Madras University. Here a survey school had been running since 1793, which was later on affiliated to the Madras University in 1858. In united province, an engineering college had been established at Roorkee in 1847 which was named afterward as the Thomson College in 1854. In Hindu College, Calcutta, a chair in Civil engineering was instituted in 1844.[9]

The wave of enthusiasm in favour of technical education has been steadily rising in the country. The technical education is considered as essential for better earnings. The history of technical education can be traced back from the year 1854. It was woods Despatch of 1854 which suggested to provide practical education to Indians which may help them to a great extent in the sphere of national development. The Hunter Commission of 1882 suggested the diversified courses of study in secondary education.[10]

Thus, there were four important engineering colleges in India in the year 1902, Roorkee, Sibapur (Bengal), Poona and Madras. The number of students attending them was 865. The development of Madras Engineering college took place between 1858 and 1862. In 1902 the total number of technical schools in India was 80 attended by 4,894 students.[11]

After 1902, Engineering and Technical education assumed a new form. Hartog Committee Report 1929 also suggested for the diversion of more boys to industrial and commercial career at the end of middle age. In 1917 Engineering classes were started in the Hindu University, Banaras and Engineering College were established at Patna, Lahore and Karachi. Between 1921 and 1937 a number of such institutions, *e.g.*, the Indian School of Mines Dhanbad, the Harcourt Technological Institute Kanpur and the School of Chemical Technology, Bombay were established. The total number of engineering institutions increased into 38 with 2,940 students up to 1947.[12]

The importance of technical education was realised still more after the Independence of the country. In 1948 the N.R. Sarkar Committee had been appointed which recommended the establishment of four big Engineering colleges, in the East, West, South and North of the country. The University education Commission also made valuable recommendation in 1949. The All India Council for Technical Education had appointed a Technical manpower committee in order to find out the number of technically trained persons needed by the country. Besides this, two more committees, *i.e.,* The Scientific Manpower Committee and the Overseas Scholarship Committee had been appointed in 1947. The All India Council for Technical Education was set up in November, 1947.[13]

The first foreign aid for the technical education was received from UNESCO in 1951 followed by the USA, the USSR, West Germany, Colombo plan etc. The Indian Institute of Science, Bangalore was raised into a University in May, 1958 which was established in 1911, owes its inception to the princely donation of the Tata Family. Besides the Indian Institute of Science, Bangalore, the Government of India had established five Indian Institute of Technology at Kharagpur in 1951, Bombay in 1958, Madras in 1959, Kanpur in 1960 and Delhi in 1963[14] and proposal is accepted by the Central Government to establish one Technological Institute in Assam during 7th Plan.

In May 1971, the Government of India created a new Department of Science and Technology under the Minister of

Planning. The first body is designed to function as the executive arm of role in the organization of technical education since the progress of the country today depends on the development of technical education. The centre has the following responsibilities :

(1) Integrated plan of development for the country as a whole.

(2) To establish institutions for special course of all India importance.

(3) To assist financially for the development of technical institutions.

(4) To watch over the progress of technical education to ensure the maintenance of high standards.[15]

The most encouraging advance in the field of Indian Education during the last decade has been in the field of technical education. In 1951 there were only 53 colleges and 89 diploma institutions for engineering and technology. But now 144 engineering colleges, 2999 diploma institutions with a total capacity of 28,000 students are functioning in the country besides 65 institutions for post-graduate degree. It is expected that by the end of 1998 India would meet the technical man power requirement with levels of facilities already created.[16]

PROBLEMS OF TECHNICAL EDUCATION

Technological development of our country suffered a lot as it is affected in several ways. In the first place, technical efficiency used at one time to be a matter of hereditary endowment, and one's birth determined one's profession. In the second place, the state except during the last 39 years never paid any serious attention to technical education. Before Independence technicians were trained mainly for satisfying administrative needs. Moreover, the training of the hand has long been neglected in favour of the intellect and we have been accustomed to place technical education third in our education and neglected technical education.[17]

During the period of this investigation, the technical education suffered a lot of problems in different point of view. some of the important problems are discussed below :

Unsuitable Curriculum

In the modern progressive society it is necessary for an efficient engineer for ensuring his advancement to keep in touch with the latest developments, besides possessing good technical knowledge. This is because the engineer has to use his technical skill for the benefit of the society. Hence, in the curriculum the inclusion of other subjects, besides the technical one is necessary. In the same way to understand the new technique, it is equally necessary for the efficient workman to have adequate knowledge of language, general science, mathematics and curriculum of technical education is of primitive nature, it does not meet the modern requirements.

Shortage of Institutions

Only a few institutions imparted technical education and the existing number falls to cope with the needs of the increasing population. There is need for its constant expansion and improvement. In this venture, co-operation of State and Central Government is of great importance. this work should proceed through a well chalked out plan. It should be got rid to development.

Shortage of Teachers

Generally, there is a dearth of properly qualified and trained teachers in the technical institutions. Low pay scales and lack of facilities do not attract talented persons to join them in teachers job. It is not possible to secure the services of efficient teachers by providing lower salaries. For example, one first class engineering graduate does not want to go into college or technical institution to be a lecturer, because he has immense chance to get any other white job in technical field. In these circumstances, it is the duty of the government to stop it and take effective steps.

Problem of Medium of Instruction

Medium is a big obstacle in the way of technical education. Now up to higher secondary level most of the students offer regional language as the medium of instruction. Books on technical and engineering subjects written in English and not published in the current language of the region. English is still the medium of instruction of these subjects. But countries like China, and Japan have produced engineering and technical books in their national languages. However, some efforts have been started in our nation also and it is hoped that soon some books on these subjects will appear in the languages generally spoken by people.[18]

Problem of Practical Work and Laboratories

The field of practical activity of technical education are the industrial institutions and workshops outside the centres of training. In the present state of acute financial position, it is not possible to provide factories and workshops in the educational institutions. Therefore, it is necessary to make arrangements for practical training in state or private factories. Only theoretical knowledge fails to develop skill and expertise among students with the result that they are not accepted by the industry.

Lack of Continuation Education

Education does not stop after getting the degree. Vocational efficiency demands training throughout life. It is very necessary to strive constantly in order to keep knowledge fresh. In this connection seminars, summer institutes and workshops etc., should be organised regularly and act as a continuous process. But it has lack, only a few institution try to organise this process.

Poor Condition of Cottage Industries

The condition of the cottage industries is very poor. Industrialisation does not mean check on the development of cottage industries. In a big industry allied cottage industries can progress a cheap rate. This would help to utilise the waste raw material properly. In this case government should encourage the people to develop the poor and establish new unit in different places.

No Provision for Refresher Course

In this modern age of scientific advancement, every day new inventions, discoveries and experiments are being made. The engineers, workers and technicians etc. have to keep, themselves fully informed with these latest developments in order to keep their knowledge up to date. But it is regretted that not a single institution provides refresher course to technicians and engineers. Arrangements should be made to impart them the desired education during their vacations or at evening centres.

Problem of Research Work

There are no more facilities for the research of technical education. The role of training should be to motivate students for original research works. This should proceed on healthy lines. Scholars should be encouraged to add to the quantum of knowledge and truth.

Lack of Co-operation and Co-ordination

Another important problem of technical education during the period of study is 'lack of co-operation and co-ordination' between Government, industry and educational institutions. This effects in the development and progress. There is need to establish proper liaison between industry and technical training institutions. The standard of technical education, and the numerical increase in the technical manpower should maintain a proper balance between them. If the government, technical institutions and industries co-operate with each other, there is no reason why the industrial development will not make rapid strides.

Administrative Difficulties

During the present study period, the problem of shortage of good administration is the result of various complex problems relating to technical education. The view that industrialization is the main source of raising standard of living in the present age, is now gaining ground. This view is dominated in the preparation of different plan. But when the administrators are responsible for industrialization, themselves lack of the knowledge of technical engineering subjects, how far industrialization will succeed can be well imagined. The Government and the Directorate of technical education can solve the administrative difficulty.

CONCLUSION

Here we can conclude the growth and development of technical education and its problems. Our programmes of technical development should not ignore the human values, which we are at present concerned to preserve. Technology in the true sense of the word *i.e.,* as an aid to man, serving the needs, is not necessarily diametrically opposed to his spiritual life. Technology should be regarded as an intellectual phenomenon, simply as the outcome of man's struggle for a higher level of civilization.[19]

Therefore, our technical education should be planned in such a way as to meet the needs of the individuals and those of the nation. The main causes of slow progress of technical education are narrow outlook, dearth of training courses, over-emphasis on cottage industries and lack of proper co-operation and co-ordination of the government and institutions. If we want to develop technical education in our society we must go ahead to remove the causes of slow progress.

NOTES

1. Chandra Kant, L.S., *Technical Education in India To-day*, Ministry of Scientific Research, New Delhi, p. 3.
2. Rawat, P.L., *History of Indian Education*, Ram Prasad and Sons, Agra, 3, 1985, p. 370.
3. *Govt. of India Science Policy Resolution, Government of India*, 1953, p. 5.
4. Lulla and Murty, *Essential Problems of Indian Education*, Lakshmi Narain Agarwal, Agra 3, 1971, p. 95.
5. *Planning Commission Draft VI Plan* (1978-83) p. 224.

6. Mukerjee, S.N., *Education in India To-day and Tomorrow*, Acharya Book Depot, Vadodara, 1976, p. 266.

7. *Ibid.*, p. 266.

8. Narian, Iqbal, *Visiting Lecture on Dilemna and Problems of Higher Education*, R-1, Gauhati University, 1-8-81.

9. Rawat, P.L., *History of Indian Education*, Ram Prasad and Sons, Agra-3, 1985, p. 372.

10. *Ibid.*

11. *Ibid.*, p. 374

12. Mukerjee, S.N., *Education in India To-day and Tomorrow*, Acharya Book Depot, Vadadara, 1976, p. 269, p. 271.

13. Rawat, P.L., *History of Indian Education*, Ramprasad and Sons, Agra 3, 1985, p. 381.

14. Mukerjee, S.N., *Education in India To-day and Tomorrow*, Acharya Book Depot, Vadodara, 1976, p. 281.

15. Chandra Kanta, L.S., *Technical Education in India Today*, Delhi, Ministry of Scientific Research and cultural Affairs, 1963, pp. 32-33.

16. (i) Rawat, P.L., *History of Indian Education*, Ram Prasad and Sons Agra 3, p. 383.

    (ii) University News December 21, 1998.

17. Lulla and Murty, *Essential Problems of Indian Education*, Lakshmi Narain Agarwal, Agra-3, p. 94.

18. Bajali College : Silver Jubilee Seminar on Science and Technical Education and Development of Human Resources Perspectives for eighties, 25.12.81, 10 a.m.

19. Kothari, D.S., *Kothari Commission* 1964-66, NCERT, Delhi, 1971, p. 707.

2

Professional Education

INTRODUCTION

After technical education professional education plays a significant role in the society. Professional education is known as vocational education and vocation is defined as “a calling to a particular occupation, business or profession.” It is an element of complete living reciprocally related to all other elements of life. Vocational education aims at training people for suitable jobs, taking into account the service conditions, the opportunities, the rewards and the special abilities required on one hand, and the abilities, aptitudes, minimum requirements, physical and emotional aspects of an individual on the other hand.[1]

Normally vocational education is viewed contemptuously when compared to cultural or liberal education, that is meant for the privileged classes of the society, where as the former is supposed to be intended for the working class. In recent years, this notion has considerably changed. Dr. H.H. Horne says “Man requires vocational education, that is, cultural at the bottom and cultural education, that is, vocational at the top.”[2]

Professional education is commendable because of its desire for improving the condition of life. It enables one not only to earn his livelihood but also to trains him for discharging the duties of his future occupation more efficiently. Vocational education was formerly confined to some learned profession only.

HISTORICAL BACKGROUND

Vocational education was quite prevalent in ancient India, when it was transmitted as a part of family education from one generation to another generation *e.g.,* Brahman's Vedas and rituals; Kshatriyas' military skills; Baishyas'-trade, navigation, etc., and other caste system that had evolved in ancient times was based purely on the system of vocation they followed.[3]

Indian Education system was influenced by the policy of the East India Company. There were no more record of professional education in ancient India. For the treatment of sufferers ancient medicine system was applied. Vaidyas were the main persons for the treatment. In Gurukula system, Gurus were the all in all for the students of ancient India. Yogas were the main item for the relief of any kind of disease. Tantra, Mantra were also applied in ancient medicine system. "Bana aushadi" was the chief medicine of the ancient India. All rules and regulations were controlled by the Headman and the Gurus. Most of the decisions of crime were settled by the kings' court and their ministers. Ministers were the powerful persons of that time.[4]

In modern Indian history of education we know that the company needed some Indian clerks and officials for its various departments in order to mange their affairs well. The company stood in need of doctors for the army, Judges and pleaders for the courts. There were the branches of professional education in the education system at the beginning of the 19th century.

Modern Medical education was introduced in India for the first time in Bengal, Bombay and Madras. In 1826 classes of medicine were started in Banaras Sanskrit college and Calcutta Madrasah. These institutions provided education in Ayurvedic, 'Yunani' and European Medical system. But after 1835 education in Ayurvedic, 'Yunani' system was discontinued and it was decided that education would be provided only in Western medical system.[5]

The Native Medical school had been founded in Bombay in

1826 and medical classes had been started in Poona College. A medical school was established at Madras for training of apprentices for lower post in 1835. It was raised to the status of Medical college and was finally merged into the University of Madras. The medium of instruction was English.[6]

British rules keeping the entire educational policy in view, introduced European Medical system which could be learnt only through the medium of English. As a matter of fact, a controversy had emerged about oriental field as well. But the policy of westernization was enunciated by Lord Macaulay, and announcement of Lord Bentinck considerably influenced medical inherent dislike of the work of dissecting the corpse, but Madhusudhan Gupta, a medical student gave the lead in this field by dissecting a corpse in Calcutta. Again in 1844 Indian students were sent to England for acquiring knowledge in the Western system of medicine.[7]

The Trained Doctors would usually be employed in Government and Municipal Board Hospital or in some big companies or factories, or would start individual practice. By the year 1902 four Medical Colleges were established in India at Calcutta, Madras, Bombay and Lahore. Besides these colleges, there were some medical schools as well. The total students of medical science in medical colleges and schools, in 1902 were 1,466 and 2,727 respectively.[8]

Medical science showed a marked progress during the period of 1903-50. The Indian people realised the immense scope for medical science in the country. During 1946-47 there were only 26 Medical colleges and 25 medical school in India. The Medical Council Act was passed in 1933 and Indian Medical Council was founded.[9]

After Independence the Government of India appointed University Education Commission. The Commission has put forth the following recommendations concerning the progress in the sphere of medical education :

(1) Medical colleges should admit a maximum number of hundred students;

(2) All departments of study which need hospital facilities should be located in the same campus;

(3) There should be provision of ten beds for per students admitted to the colleges;

(4) Training should also be acquired in rural centres both at the undergraduate and post-graduate stages;

(5) Provision of post-graduate training should be made in those colleges which have adequate staff and equipment;

(6) More importance should be attached to public health, Engineering and Nursing;

(7) Indigenous medical systems should be encouraged and

(8) History of medicine with special reference to Indian systems should be taught in the first Degree course in Medicine.[10]

The number of medical colleges were increased form 30 in 1950-51 to 87 in 1965-66 enabling the intake to be raised form 2,500 to 10,625.[11]

But, because of the rapid growth of population the doctor's populations ratio remained constant at 1 : 5880. By 1976, the doctor population ratio might reach up to 1 : 3500. Facilities for post-graduate education would be increased so as to raise the present intake of 800 up to 400 by the end of 4th Plan. At the same time the facilities have also to be enlarged for middle level personal such as nurses, midwives, health visitors and sanitary Inspectors.[12]

Legal education plays a wide role in the history of professional education. For legal education in India Britishers had established the Calcutta Madrasah and the Sanskrit college, Banaras, where Law pertaining to the main Indian races, Hindus, Muslims, might be taught and when the East Indian Company might draw their supply of Judges and pleaders for their courts.

A professor was appointed in the Hindu college, Calcutta for law in 1842. In 1857 with the incorporation of Calcutta University and owing to certain difficulties of starting law college under it, the classes in Jurisprudence could not be started until 1865. Regular classes in law could be instituted only after the establishment of Bombay and Madras University. Study of law, was by and by growing in popularity, because lawyers and judges were in great demand owing to the establishment of law courts in the country.[13]

Education in law was under the control of Universities, Department of Education and High Court respectively. Universities set up curriculum of education in law and they held examinations. Law schools and colleges were under the control of Department of education and High Court prescribed certain conditions, the fulfilment where of only could, entitle a Bachelor of Law to undertake the profession of law. Prior to this the High Courts gave their own examinations. In some provinces, examinations of 'pleader' and 'Muktar' were conducted only for matriculate candidates. The course of L.L.B. covered usually a period of two years. It took three years in some places to be completed only after graduation either in arts or in science. However, study of law during the period of 1902 and 1927 was immensely beneficial for the interest of the country. The country has produced eminent lawyers. As a matter of fact, lawyers have contributed immensely towards the achievement of our Independence in 1947. The entire market of law is overflooded today by these professionalists.[14]

During 1946-47 there were only 14 law colleges, six Universities possessed law departments and law classes conducted by six colleges affiliated to the University of Arga. Though the development of law education was broadened, the natural consequences of all this had been that there was a total lack of Research work and higher studies in the sphere of education of law.[15]

Therefore, 'obviously, we now need to recognise our law colleges and give emphasis to this subject second to none.

India's prominence and importance among Independent nations and the realisation of our national aims demand such a course of action.[16]

In this connection University Education Commission has put-forth the following recommendations :

(1) There should be reorganisation of our law colleges.

(2) The staff of the law faculties should be recruited and controlled by the Universities in the way similar to Arts and Science Faculties.

(3) A degree course covering three years in pre-legal and general studies should be required for admission to law classes.

(4) As regards special legal subjects, a three-year degree course should be offered and the last year should be given over largely to practical training.

(5) The staff in law faculty should be both whole time and part time.

(6) Law classes should be scheduled only during the regular hours of teaching.

(7) Students pursuing study of law should not undertake the study of any other subject.

(8) There should be facilities of higher education and research work in law and

(9) Improvement should be introduced in the system of examination.[17]

But in comparison of India "The minimum requirements of pre-legal training of the American Bar Association and the American Association of Law Schools in two years of college work but the best colleges of law including Harvard, Columbia, Michigan, Chicago, California and others require completion of four years degree courses in Arts and Science before admission to the law course."[18]

The interest of the Government of India diverted towards

veterinary science, veterinary science occupied a very important place in an agricultural country like India. In Lahore a veterinary college was founded in 1832, in Bombay in 1882 and at Calcutta in 1893, another veterinary school was established at Azmir but latter on it was amalgamated with the veterinary college at Lahore.

During the period of 1903-50 there was a good progress in the sphere of Veterinary science. In 1903 the Civil Veterinary Department was made available for the general public as well. Progress in Agricultural Department entailed a development in Veterinary Science. During 1902-07 the veterinary schools were abolished to be substituted by veterinary college. Consequently veterinary college were established at Madras, Patna in 1905 and 1930, and one Research Institute was established at Garh Mukteswar in U.P., in 1948, a Veterinary College had been established at Jaipur. There were Research Institutes at Izatnagar and Bangalore. The Government of U.P. established a veterinary college at Mathura. In different places of India, in order to recognise veterinary schools into college and to control the system there established an Agricultural University.[19]

Agricultural development of India is no more wide. The first attempt was made by the British Royal Agricultural Society in 1889 when it sent Dr. A. Voilkar to India to study Indian agriculture. He visited India in 1890, an agricultural conference was held and several recommendations were also made in this respect. As a result, a number of experts on agricultural field were appointed. Lord Curzon gave an impetus to agricultural education. He enunciated a new policy on agriculture and created a central Institute at Pusa. He also laid down the principle that every important province in India must have its own agricultural college.[20]

Royal Commission on Agriculture was appointed in 1928, and as a result of which the Imperial Council of Agricultural Research was incorporated in 1929. Indian council of Agricultural Research, Indian Institute of Food Technology, Central Agricultural Marketing Department and Indian Dairy Research Institute are some of the Institutes for agricultural Research in addition to that, there are facilities for higher and post-Graduate training in certain studies in agricultural science in some of the Indian Universities.[21]

University Education Commission of 1948 recommends some ideas regarding agricultural education in India. This commission suggests that agricultural education should be recognised as a major national issue, the study of agriculture in different stages of education.

Again the Commission of 1948 is of opinion that to avoid famine in the country, the production of food must be doubled in the next 15 years and maintain an adequate growth rate thereafter. This programme of education for agriculture will be based on three main elements — research or the development of the appropriate technology, extension at the communication of the technology to practising farmers, and training of the needed personnel.[22]

In order to develop programmes of agriculture the Commission has put forth the following recommendations :

(1) to set up a number of agricultural universities with integrated programmes of research training and extension,

(2) to attract talented students, researchers and teachers to agriculture,

(3) to develop programmes of agricultural research, training and extention in other universities and institutions of higher education,

(4) to improve agricultural colleges,

(5) to establish agricultural polytechnics to train agricultural technicians,

(6) to give a certain orientation to agriculture and rural problems in the education system as a whole,

(7) to develop agricultural extension programmes, and particularly to establish primary extension centres and

(8) to associate successful and progressive farmers closely with the agricultural universities, colleges, polytechnics and primary extension centres and to give them adequate status and facilities.[23]

At least one agricultural college should be established in each state the Commission said. An academic relationship between some of the agricultural universities and the I.I.T's[24] should be developed.

Besides the above mentioned practical education, there were certain other branches of it which prepared students for the economic aspects of their lives, *i.e.,* Teaching, Forestry, Art and Cottage industry, Commerce etc. Many colleges and schools had been established for the training of teachers of different level. There were training colleges for women candidates as well. Some Universities were running classes of B.Ed. and M.Ed. The Institute of Education, Bombay, Central Institute of Education, Delhi, Centre of Advance Study (Education), Boroda and Centre of Advance Study Bhubaneswar provided facilities in research work.

PROBLEMS OF PROFESSIONAL EDUCATION

Standardization of Curriculum

One of the important problem of professional education is standardization of curriculum. In present situation, the prescribed syllabus of professional and vocational education does not suit our society. Present curriculum has no practical value at all. After completion of the courses the students who qualify themselves for the degree are not fit to work in the field. It hampers the progress of professional education.

Not Related with the Profession

Our present educational system is not related to the profession concerned. Professional ethics of the students are not related with the system of our education. Present curriculum of our education system is depended on books, because books are the chief career of present education.

Shortage of Teachers

During recent years, there is a grave concern for the shortage of teachers. This is mainly due to the large demand for professional personnel in the country. In addition there is a shyness for the professional scholars to man the teaching profession. This is the result of many socio-economic factors. Teaching is considered a job of second importance, socially, economically and culturally. Teaching is not a mechanical process, it requires a man of character, dynamic talent of imagination.

Unsuitable Professional Institution

Professional institution must also provide the necessary facilities for continuing education of the practising professionals. These institutions must hold frequent discussions on the problem of professionals encountered in day to day work as they will be not only useful but enlighten young professional institutions that are not more helpful for education.

Unsuitable text Books

Professional education suffers from lack of good text books. Experienced and reputed teachers evince no interest in this respect. It has lowered the standard of teaching and education. There is an urgent need to put a check on superfluous instructional materials. Universities can render useful service in this direction.

Lack of Suitable Equipments

Another burning problem of professional education is shortage of suitable equipments and other materials. Lack of funds is one of the greatest hardles in the way of professional education. Government is tendered for supply of equipments and other accessories for the laboratory, classroom and library. The supplier supplies low standard of scientific equipments and other materials for the institutions. After using these for one or two times, most of these materials are damaged and students suffer for the whole year.

Problem of Braindrain

From our country, a large number of students go abroad for higher education and most of them settle there, because of good emoluments, attraction and glamour. This has presented a problem of braindrain before the country and is a great national loss. This requires providing similar facilities to the students within the country. The idea of establishing major universities put forth by Kothari Commission, 1964-66, is a good step to check this problem.

Problem of Administration

In the case of development of professional institutions Government is always unminded in its proper development. Institutions are always Government institutions, all administrations and control in the hand of Government, central and state. In most cases governments are responsible for the proper development of professional education. Particularly in the case of appointment of teachers, different irrelevant situations occur and students suffer a lot, which is not fulfilled for the whole session. Government should take interest to solve the problem in time.

The over all assessment of professional education in the past shows that the expansion was considerably less than what it should have been. The reasons for the slow pace of vocational education may be stated as follows :

(1) Lack of earnestness on the part of alien government;

(2) Slow pace of structural development;

(3) Lack of sufficient demand on the part of public;

(4) Scornful view of vocational pursuits etc.

CONCLUSION

It is, in short, the growth and development of professional education in our country are slow in nature. Professional education gains prominence in the context of marking the citizens of our country as creative and productive as possible.

They will be enabled to fit into a calling according to their abilities, aptitudes, interests and tastes and thus it will become benefiting members of the society, who benefit the society with their own creativity and productivity. The world of today is marching fast on the path of materialistic progress and prosperity. For an underdeveloped country like India there is no short cut of progress but to utilise the human resources for its rapid socio-economic growth and prosperity of the masses who are steeped object poverty. Institutions are established to solve the great rush of enrollment but due to shortage of different part professional education became unsuitable in nature.

Here we can mention the opinion of Education Commission of 1964-66 that,

About fifty year later we find that the overall picture has increased only slightly and the proportion of the students at the University stage enrolled in all courses of Professional education is only 23 per cent of the total population.[25]

NOTES

1. Brubacher, J.S., *A History of Problems of Education*, New York Mc Graw Hill Book Co., Inc, 1947, p. 112.
2. Lulla, B.P., and Murty, S.K., *Problems of Indian Education*, Lakshmi Narain Agarwal, Agra-3, 1971, p. 73.
3. Mukerjee, R.K. (Dr.), *Ancient Indian Education*, Macmillan and Co, London (1947), p. 21.
4. Altekar, A.S. (Dr.), *Education in Ancient India*, Nand Kishore Bros. Banaras (1948), p. 185.
5. Rawat, P.L., *History of Education in India*, Ram Prasad and Sons, Agra 3, 1985, p. 371.
6. *Ibid.*, p. 371.
7. *Ibid.*, p. 373.
8. *Ibid.*, p. 373.
9. *Ibid.*, p. 378.
10. Govt. of India, *Report of the University Education Commission* Vol. I, 1949.
11. Chaube and Chaube, *Problems of Indian Education*, Vikash Publishing House, Delhi 1, 1981, p. 181.

12. 'Souvenir', *All India Gynocological Congress*, Vol.XI, Guwahati, 1979, p. 42.
13. Bhatia and Arora, *History of Education in India*, D.P. Rai and Sons, Agra, 1981, p. 187.
14. Rawat, P.L., *History of Indian Education*, Ram Prasad and Sons, Agra-3, 1985, p. 377.
15. *Ibid.*, p. 377.
16. Govt. of India, *Radhakrishnan Commission Report (U.E.)*, 1948, p. 260.
17. *Ibid.*, U.E.C., 1948, p. 260.
18. *Ibid.*, p. 260.
19. Rawat, P.L., *History of Indian Education*, Ram Prasad and Sons, Agra-3, 1985, p. 373.
20. Dutta, D., *History of Indian Education*, B. Prakashani, Calcutta, 1969, p. 10.
21. Association of Indian Universities, *University News*, Vol. 1, July, 1979, p. 13.
22. Kothari, D.S., *Report of the Education Commission*, 1964-66, NCERT, 1971, p. 639.
23. *Ibid.*, p. 640.
24. I.I.T, Indian Institute of Technology.
25. Kothari, D.S., *Kothari Commission Report 1964-66*, NCERT, 1971, p. 686.

3

Women Education

INTRODUCTION

The destiny of a nation is moulded and fashioned through its education and in this, the education of women has a strategic importance. The significance of the education of women can not be over-emphasised. There cannot be an educated nation without educated women. If general education had to be limited to men or to women, that opportunity should be given to women, for them it would most surely be passed on to the next generation.[1(a)]

In a democratic system, the place of women like men is of great importance. These days, women are conscious about their rights and obligations. In India, the percentage of women's education is on the increase; at present it is about 39.19 per cent.[1(b)] In the eight plan, the national government had launched a major scheme for the development and improvement of women's education in the country. This will help to develop proper awareness in them. This is very necessary for the success of democracy.[2]

Mother is the first educator of a child. From birth to school age, the home environment and association of other members of the family play a significant role in developing proper attitudes among them. But much more important is the influence of mother on the child. She is responsible for his or her upbringing and care. Therefore, it is very necessary that a mother is imbued with good qualities and acts as model. She should be an efficient citizen conscious of her rights and responsibilities.

Thus, education of women is of great importance in our national and social life and we have to be very careful in this respect. It is the duty of our society and the government to provide adequate facilities for the education of women because if we educate a girl, we educate the whole family.

HISTORICAL BACKGROUND

Women education in our country has passed through several stages of development. In ancient India both men and women had an access to education. In the Vedic age equality was given to women. They enjoyed special opportunity and freedom. Both boys and girls received education in 'Ashrams' and 'Gurukulas'. In the Rigveda mention was made of the 'Rishikas' like 'Romasa' Lopamudra, Apala, Kadru, Visvavara, Ghosa and others. Women sages were called 'Rishikas' and 'Brahmabadhinis'.[3] But latter time's education of women got low priority and the introduction of early marriage acted as a previous pitfall on the way of education. Gradually, their privileges were curtailed and society tended to be a patriarchal one and education remained in the hands of religious people who did not allow co-education. The Upanayana ceremony which marked the initiation of a child into a study of the Vedas was performed for boys as well as for girls. The position of women was one of the authority of honour in latter Vedic period.[4]

During the days of he Muslims the women rotted behind the 'purdah' and were not allowed to mix with men, and education of girls was restricted to higher families only.[5]

But on the other hand, we find that during the rule of the East Indian Company female education was the most neglected subject. There were no separate schools for girls and the number of girls students attending boys schools were negligible.[6]

The company's rule hardly made any provision for state owned girls school. Then it was purely a concern of the

Missionaries. But they could not weather the strong opposition against both social and religious. A number of private schools were conducted by the British officials and non-officials on their own. The most important institution of this type was the 'Bethune school', Calcutta, which was founded in 1849 by Mr. J.E.D. Bethune, the Legal Member of the Supreme Council of the Government of India. This school gave impetus to Indians to start similar institutions in the country.[7]

'May' and 'Carey' were associated with opening of a number of schools during this period. The Indian Women had a great defender of their rights in Raja Ram Mohan Ray and the 'Brahmo Samaj' has a record of conspicuous services for their advancement.[8]

The woods Despatch of 1854 recognised for the first time that the Government should give 'frank and cordial support' to female education and take effective measures for expansion of it. But unfortunately the government did practically nothing to implement the recommendations of this Despatch regarding female education.[9]

In 1877 Calcutta University for the first time allowed girl candidates to appear in the Matriculation examination. In 1878 the college classes were started in the 'Bethune school for girls'. In 1883, Bombay University threw all University examinations open to girls. It may be mentioned here that the two Indian ladies Srimati Chandramukhi Basu and Kadambini Basu passed the B.A. examination from Calcutta University in 1882.[10]

The Indian Education Commission of 1882, while examining the question of girls' education, remarked 'Female education is still in an extremely backward condition and needs to be fostered in every legitimate way.' It recommended that it should receive a larger share of public funds. As a result state funds were spent more freely on girls' education. By the end of 1901-02 there were 12 colleges, 467 secondary schools and 5628 primary schools for girls, but the total enrollment in all educational institutions was 4,47,470 only.[11]

During 1902-17 some active steps were taken by the Government for the improvement of women education. In 1904 Mrs. Annie Besant established the Central Hindu Girls' School at Banaras with the object of imparting Western education to girls. In 1916, the first Medical College, Lady Hardinge College, Delhi was established for the fair sex in the country. The S.N.D.T. Women's University was also established in the same year.[12]

The period from 1917 to 1947 is one of the significant period of development in India. Among the earliest of Women's Organizations was the Women's Indian Association founded in 1917 under the guidance of Dr. Annie Besant and Mrs. Margaret Cousins. In 1925, the National Council of Women was established. It has now fourteen state branches and is affiliated to the International Council of Women.[13]

The greatest impetus to women's cause, however, came from the national movement launched by Mahamanab Mahatma Gandhi. His appeal to Indian mothers for the country's cause fired their spirit of nationalism. Numerous public gatherings of women were annually held to discuss the programmes of social and educational reconstruction. The Sarda Act has made child marriage illegal throughout the country. The first All India Women Conference was held in 1927 sharing in the ideals and programmes of National Council of Women. It not only reiterated demands for equality of educational opportunities but also agitated for the education of women and amelioration of their social position.[14]

The women's movement in contemporary Europe and the USA inspired the women of India to fight for their emancipation and knit them together in close organisations. It included the economic and social impact of the two world wars, the national awakening in India, a progress in economic and social matters, and finally the winning of freedom and partition of the country on August 15, 1947.[15]

The Radhakrishnan Commission of 1948 recommended that

the ordinary amenities and decencies of life should be provided for women in colleges ordinarily planned for men and that there should be no curtailment of educational opportunities for women rather great increase. The commission stressed that 'They shall not try to imitate men, but shall desire as good education as women, as men get as men. Women's and Men's education should have many elements in common, but should not in general be identical in all respect as is usually the case today."[16]

A number of Education Commission and Committees appointed in different states of the country expressed their views about women's education and put forth suggestions with regards to its promotion. Higher education developed immensely and Women began to be absorbed in many vacancies in Hospitals, Schools and various offices.

S.N.D.T. WOMEN UNIVERSITY

S.N.D.T. Women University owes its origin to a school for Hindu Widows started by Prof. D.K. Karve at Poona in 1896. This small school very soon developed into a big institution with the combination of a hostel, a primary school, a secondary school and a training school for primary teachers. The institution was so well managed that many parents began keeping even their unmarried daughter in the hostel.[17]

This encouraged Prof. Karve to devise a new scheme of higher education for Indian girls. He fervently believed that the educational needs of men and women are entirely different since they have to play different role in life. As a result, the Indian Women's University was started in 1916 and has been shaped according to Prof. Karve's ideals. The University is in some ways a unique national institution for the education of women. It attracts students not only from different states of India, but also from abroad. The headquarters of the University were removed to Bombay in 1930. It was named after Srimati Nathibi Damodardeo Thackersey, the mother of a famous

Bombay merchant who donated a large sum to the University in her memory to serve the society for women.[18]

NATIONAL COUNCIL FOR WOMEN'S EDUCATION, 1959

National Council for Women Education was set up in 1959, and was reconstituted in 1964. In addition to the Chairman and the secretary, it consists of twenty seven members. The council discharges the following functions :

(1) To advise the central government with regard to the problem of women's education.

(2) To fix up the policy, programme, priorities and goals for its expansion and development.

(3) To take suitable steps for eliciting the co-operation of voluntary organisations.

(4) To organise seminars, take up surveys and other research works for the improvement of girls' education in the country.

(5) To make periodic evaluation of the progress of women's education.[19]

DURGABAI DESHMUKH COMMITTEE, 1959

Durgabai Deshmukh Committee appointed by the national government with regard to the education of girls gave the following recommendations :

(1) The central and state governments should give priority to the education of girls.

(2) In the central ministry of education, a department of women's education should be created.

(3) For proper education of girls, a director of women's education should be appointed in each state.

(4) Co-education should be properly organised at higher level of education.

(5) The University Grants Commission should specify a definitc amount separately for the education of girls.

(6) In the first phase of development, provision of free education should be made for girls up to class VIII.

(7) Facilities in the choice of optional subjects should be made available for girls

(8) Girls should get training facilities on a liberal basis.

(9) Education of girls should be given due encouragement in rural areas.

(10) A large number of seats in various services should be reserved for them.

(11) Programmes for the development of adult women's education should be properly initiated and encouraged.[20]

HANSA MEHTA COMMITTEE REPORT, 1962

Hansa Mehta Committee was appointed by the National Council for women education in 1962 under the Chairmanship of Smti Hansa Mehta, to examine carefully the differentiation of curriculum for boys and girls at all stages of education. The committee analysed the issue threadbare and made the following recommendations :

(1) There is need to make differentiation in the curriculum on the basis of sex

(2) At Higher Secondary level, home science is a useful subject for girls but it should not be made compulsory.

(3) Music, drawing, painting and fine arts are the subjects of interest for girls and, therefore, proper facilities for their teaching should exist in educational institutions.

(4) Girls in sufficient number should be encouraged to offer science and mathematics subjects.

(5) In place of physical education, hand-work should form a part of girls' education.[21]

BHAKTAVATSALAM COMMITTEE REPORT, 1963

In 1963 the National Council for Women Education appointed a committee under the Chairmanship of Sri M. Bhaktavatsalam, the then Chief Minister of Madras, to look into the causes for the lack of public support, particularly in rural areas for girls' education and to enlist public co-operation. The committee made the following recommendations :

(1) The government and the public both should act jointly, realise their responsibilities and proceed in a planned manner with regard to the education of girls in future.

(2) Co-education should be made popular at the primary level.

(3) Married educated women's service should be utilised on part time basis in the teaching work.

(4) State Governments should enlighten the public with regard to the education of girls by organising conferences, seminars and display of audio-visual material.

(5) Similarly, the central government should provide economic help liberally for the education of women.

(6) In rural areas, social education centres for women should be established in large numbers.

(7) Facilities of attractive emoluments, living accommodation and conveyance charges, etc., should be made available to women teachers.

(8) The inspection of schools should be made regular and effective.

(9) In teachers' training centres seats should be reserved for women student teachers hailing from rural areas.

(10) A functional curriculum should be evolved for educating adult women.[22]

MAIN RECOMMENDATIONS OF KOTHARI COMMISSION, 1964-66

Kothari Commission, 1964-66 had suggested to launch two

types of developmental plans with regard to women's education. The details are given below :

(a) *General Work Plan* : The general work plan deals with the progress of girls' education at different stages of education. Under this it had suggested that education of both boys and girls should proceed on the basis of equality without any discrimination and facilities of part time work should be provided to women in leisure hours. For late marriages, they should be engaged in some socially useful productive work. We cannot overlook the place and importance of women in national reconstruction. They can contribute significantly in the field of teaching, nursing and social service.

(b) *Special Programmes* : It provides a long-term plan for the development of women's education in the country. The main purpose of the plan is to remove the existing inequalities between the education of boys and girls at the earliest. For this, special provisions are to be made in budget allocations. The central and state governments should take suitable steps for their implementation. It is also necessary to seek co-operation of the general public in this respect.

Apart from the above, for undertaking the posts of responsibilities, effective education of girls is essential. Facilities of scholarships and other financial assistance should be made available to them on a liberal basis at all stages of education. There is an urgent need for establishing a national institute of women's education at the centre with its branches in states for its development and progress.[23]

NATIONAL COMMITTEE ON WOMEN'S EDUCATION, 1970

A National Committee on Women's Education was constituted for reviewing the progress of women's education in the country and suggesteding measures for further development and improvement. The main recommendations of the committee are the following :

(1) Priority should be given to women's education in the

future programmes of the development of education in the country.

(2) Discrimination between the education of boys and girls should be curbed and both should expand on a equal footing.

(3) The national government should encourage states to launch various programmes associated with the development of women's education.

(4) Proper facilities and protection should be provided to woman teachers serving in the rural areas.[24]

As a result of the appointment of these committees and commissions, the overall figures of girls' education at all stages during recent years showed an impressive advance. During 1971-72 there were 4,68,696 women students in the Higher Educational institutions and total enrollment of male and female were 20,65,041 only. But in the year 1990-91 enrollment was increased up to 14,36,887 out of 44,25,247 total enrollment in the institutions for higher education in our country.[25]

TABLE 1

Table shows the Enrollment of Students in the Higher Educational Institutions and enrollment of women and their Percentage from 1971-72 to 1990-91

Year	Total Enrollment	Women Enrollment	Percentage of women students
1	2	3	4
1971-72	20,65,041	4,68,696	22.7
1973-74	22,34,385	5,20,825	23.3
1974-75	23,66,541	5,53,009	23.4
1975-76	24,26,109	5,95,162	24.5
1976-77	24,31,563	6,27,346	25.8
1979-80	26,48,579	7,89,042	26.0
1980-81	27,52,437	7,48,525	27.2
1981-82	29,52,066	8,16,704	27.7

1	2	3	4
1982-83	31,33,093	8,80,156	28.1
1983-84	33,07,649	9,40,253	28.4
1984-85	34,04,096	9,92,139	29.1
1985-86	35,70,897	10,58,612	29.6
1986-87	36,81,870	11,25,304	30.6
1987-88	38,14,417	11,95,073	31.3
1988-89	39,47,922	12,51,491	31.7
1989-90	42,46,878	13,67,495	32.2
1990-91	44,25,247	14,36,887	32.5

Source : University Grants Commission Report for 1981-82, 1988-89, 1990-91.

TABLE 2

Table shows the Number of Colleges for Women only from 1974-75 to 1990-91

Year	College
1974-75	506
1975-76	528
1976-77	543
1979-80	577
1980-81	609
1981-82	624
1982-83	647
1983-84	676
1984-85	712
1985-86	741
1987-88	771
1988-89	824
1989-90	851
1990-91	874

Source : University Grants Commission Report 1981-82, 1988-89, 1990-91

One of the most disheartening features in the disparity between literary percentage of boys and girls in different stages. The percentage of literacy in 1901 was 0.80 per cent of women and rates was 9.83, and in 1991 was 39.19 and rates was 52.19.[26]

TABLE 3

Table shows the Percentage of Literacy of Female from 1901 to 1991

Year	Rates	Females
1901	9.83	0.80
1911	10.56	1.05
1921	12.21	1.81
1931	15.59	2.93
1941	24.90	7.30
1951	34.44	7.93
1961	34.44	12.95
1971	39.45	18.69
1981	46.74	24.88
1991	52.19	39.19*

Source : University News December 1, 1982, p. 720.
Education in Emerging India (J.C. Agarwal) Doaba House Delhi, 1994.

*Approximate.

PROBLEMS OF WOMEN EDUCATION

Before going to discuss about the problems of Women education of our country we can mention here the recommendations of University Education Commission, 1949. The University Education Commission discussed at length the problems of women education at college and University stages and put forth following recommendations in this regard :

(1) The ordinary amenities and decencies of life should be provided for women in colleges originally planned for men but to which women are being admitted in increasing numbers.

(2) There should be no curtailment in educational opportunities for women, but rather a great increase.

(3) There should be intelligent educational guidance by qualified men and women, to help women to get a clearer view of their real educational interests, to the end that they shall not try to imitate man, but shall desire as good education as women as men get as men — women's and men's education should have many elements in common, but should not in general, be identical in all respects as is usually the case of today.

(4) Woman students in general should be helped to see their normal places in a normal society, both as citizens and as women and to prepare for it, and college programmes should be so designed that it will be possible for them to do so.

(5) Through educational council and by example the prevailing prejudice against study of home economics and home management should be overcome.

(6) Standards of custody and social responsibility should be emphasised on the part of men in mixed colleges.

(7) Where new colleges are established to serve both men and women students they should be truely co-educational institutions with as much thought and consideration given to the life needs of women as to those of men. Except as such colleges come into existence, there are no valid criteria for comparing segregated education with co-education.

(8) Women teachers should be paid the same salaries as men teachers for equal work.[27]

The Women education of our country has suffered form the following problems :

Problems of Co-education

In the present progressive age it is desirable that men and women hold the same status in society. Generally co-education means education of both boys and girls together in the same institution. But there are some problems now also. In ancient Hindu system co-education was not at all in existences but at present co-education is popular in our society. Though it is popular in our present society, people always try to establish new separate institutions for their girls, because girl students faced some problems in the co-educational institution. As regard hostels, men hostels have better facilities than women hostels. The girl students are kept under control in early years, and in the later years also they are not permitted to go out after 6 o'clock in the evening.

Problems of Institutions

In comparison to general colleges, women colleges and other institutions are few in number. Women students are enrolled in the co-educational institutions. In some places due to shortage of institutions women students withdrew their education and fall in the period of wastage. They have a tendency to get their daughters married as soon as possible after they attain a certain age. Thus, conservative attitude of the people especially in rural areas is a difficult problem.

Economic Problems

Most of the people of our country depend on agriculture and small business, like rope, basket and mat making. Boys and girls are enrolled in the educational institution, but the parents decide at last, to drop their girls from the educational institutions. Because in our social position education of boys is more essential than girls for future. Low income source has hampered the development of education of women.

Dearth of Female Teacher

Another stumbling block on the path of female education is the dearth of female teachers. Many people do not subscribe to the idea of appointing male teachers in female institutions. On the other hand, it is hard to find a teacher who can handle all the subjects of curriculum. Another case, some of the institutions established completely under rural set up and the appointment of female teachers create a awkward situation for the residential accommodation.

Early Marriage

Another social problem is the marriage of the girls in early stage. Most of the qualified grooms search for educated girls of teenage. Some of the parents think about the problem of daughter, in their mind girls are the social burden for future. They decide to give marriage their teenaged daughter to a handsome youth as early as possible. After the completion of school education, the next duty of the girl is to marry anyone according to their parent's will.

Household Responsibilities

The main responsibility of the backwardness of female eduction rest with the Guardians. Generally when they go to the field of some other places in search of money, they compel their daughters stay at home to look after the household activities like cooking, cleaning, clothmaking, spinning, weaving etc. Most of the economically backward family send their daughter as maid servants to other reputed family of urban area for economic benefit.

Problem of Accommodation and Communication

Accommodation for girl students is not available in all educational institutions. Most of the people live in villages and they need residential facilities in college campus. Hostel seats are limited in number, all girls will not be able to get hostel facilities. On the other hand, road communication from one place to another place is not more satisfactory till now.

Therefore, some of the interested girls are deprived of Higher education.

Problem of Curriculum

The system of women's education, its curriculum and programme are the same as prescribed for men's education. The progress so far achieved clearly shows that still greater success can be attained if the subjects of study are changed to suit the taste and temperament of women and prove useful to them. Though men and women equal in status but some curriculum hinder the system of women education.

CONCLUSION

Here we can conclude, the growth and development of women education of our country. Though education and training are the keys to entry into the areas of progress in all spheres of life, women continue to be greatly handicapped. Educational achievements of women are significally low in our present society. Formal education for girls has not been suitable either to their traditional roles or to the performance of new types of roles appropriate for women in a changing society. Mass poverty is stumbling block in the way of women's education. It is the utmost urgency and necessity that all these hindrances should be removed from the way of women education. In rural areas, centres of secondary and higher education should be opened for girls, and special extension classes should be started for social education among adult women. Social status and education of women are inter-dependent. The spread of education among women leads to improvement in their status which in turn leads to further educational, social and economic development.

NOTES

1(a). Thakersy, P., *Education of women,* Ministry of Education and Youth Services, Govt. of India, 1970, p. V.

1(b). Government of India : Census Report 1991.

2. Manager of Publication, *National Council for Women's Education*, New Delhi, 1985, p. 20.

3. Alteker, A.S., *Education in Ancient India*, 1948, p. 3.

4. Keay, F.E., *Indian Education in Ancient and Later Times*, Bombay, Oxford University Press, 1942, p. 7.
5. Hussain, Yusuf, Education in the Muslim Period, p. XXI.
6. Mukerjee, S.N., *Education in India Today and Tomorrow*, Acharya Book Depot, Vadodava, 1979, p. 232.
7. *Ibid.*, p. 232.
8. Das, L., *Education in Assam*, United Das Publishers, Guwahati 1971, p. 51.
9. Rawat, P.L., *History of Indian Education*, R.P. Sons, Agra, 1985, p. 439.
10. Das, L., *Education in Assam*, United Das Publishers, Guwahati 1978, p. 52.
11. Mukherjee, S.N., *Education in India Today and Tomorrow*, Acharya Book Depot, Vadodara, 1979, p. 233.
12. *Ibid.*, p. 234.
13. *Ibid.*, p. 235.
14. *Ibid.*, p. 235.
15. *Ibid.*, p. 235.
16. Government of India, *Report of the University Education Commission*, 1949, p. 240.
17. Thackersey, P., *Education of women*, Ministry of Education and Youth Services, Govt. of India, 1970.
18. Mukerjee, S.N., *Education in India To-day and Tomorrow*, Acharya Book Depot, Vadodara, 1973, pp. 510-11.
19. Mukerjee, S.N., *Education in India To-day and Tomorrow*, Acharya Book Depot, Vadodara, 1979, p. 239.
20. Govt. of India, Durgabai Deshmukh Committee, Report, 1959.
21. Kohli, V.K., *Current Problems of Indian Education*, Krishna Brothers, Jullunder, 1974, p. 47.
22. Sharma, A.P., *Contemporary Problems of Education*, Vani Educational Books, 1968, p. 201.
23. Kothari, D.S., *Kothari Commission*, 1964-66, NCERT, 1971, p. 241.
24. Manager of Publication, *Report of National Committee on Women's Education*, New Delhi, 1970.
25. UGC, University Grnats Commission Report, 1990-91.
26. (i) A.I.U., University News, December 1, 1982, p. 720.
    (ii) Agarwal, J.C., : *Education in Emerging India*, Doaba House Delhi 1994.
27. Government of India (1948-49), *The Report of the University Education Commission*, Government of India Press, 1950.

4
Science Education

INTRODUCTION

Mankinds desire to know the unknown that is never satisfied. To satisfy their thirst for knowledge, they accept the domination of science. Science will not step down from its high throne as long as desire to penetrate the secret and unknown regions of knowledge remain. Civilization has reached its present ebb fully on account of science. It has brought about a great change in the present age. There is no sphere of life which has not been affected by science. The quick development of science changed the face of the earth beyond expectations. With the help of science, man conquered time and distance, ailments and sufferings and they became the master of their surroundings.

The importance of science education need not be weighed and in fact, cannot be weighed, and it is also impossible to enumerate the attainments of science. The growth of scientific knowledge has been so fast that it is impossible for observers to keep track of all these.

Science has added a new dimension to education and to its role in the life of nation, but central to all this is the quality of education. If science is poorly taught and badly learnt, it is little more than burdening the mind with dead information, and it could degenerate even into a new superstition. What we desperately need is improvement in the standard and quality of science education at all levels in the country. Strengthening university, science and research must be treated as a fundamental national goal. Strong and progressive Universities constitute the foundation of all research and development effort of the nation. To achieve quality in science education and research demand serious and sustained effort, full and vigorous government and public support, a relentless pursuit of excellence and above all it needs determination, hard work and dedication.[1]

The rapid growth of scientific knowledge also testifies to the position, science holds and necessitates and concerted approach of all who want to march ahead with time. The rapid rate of growth is indicated by the doubling time of only ten years during which period the total scientific knowledges accumulated equals that during the last hundred years since the beginning of the scientific revolution.[2]

The next result of this monstrous growth of scientific knowledge is that it has pervaded all walks of human life and has not only changed the human behaviour from materialistic point of view but has deep impact of man's ideas and thinking too.[3]

HISTORICAL BACKGROUND

Modern age is the age of scientific advancement and technological progress. Since the advent of science, the entire thinking, mode of living, working conditions and systems of education have undergone a revolutionary change. As a result of scientific development, (discoveries and inventions) the mysteries of nature are being revealed to making every day and things considered so far the symbols of supernatural powers are gradually passing under the control of man. He has not only harnessed science is controlling physical powers but now he is asking for a complete mastery of nature. He has already conquered the earth, the mountains and the oceans, and now looking forward with a degree of success to the moon or be marsh. On this planet called earth, the technological advancement has diverted the whole stream of man's life.[4]

Under such circumstances all these developments must surely affect his education.

Scientific advancement has changed the pattern of education all over the world. In highly advanced countries like United States, Great Britain or Soviet Russia, Science and Technology have advanced to such a degree that not only education but the entire human life has also been revolutionised. India is far more behind in scientific progress in comparison to some of the countries of the West and Technological growth is rather a recent phenomenon in this country.[5]

If we study the ancient history of our nation science and technology were more wide than the present time. In this case we may mention the different kind of architectural design, weather forecast machine, time measuring instrument etc. The real development of science occurs in modern age which is known as the age of science.

Modern education began in India after the seventeenth century. The aim of British empire was to spread the Western culture and science in India. Here we can mention the name of 'Lord Macaulay' the law member of the council of Governor General. He was a scholar of English literature and a fine orator. But he always advocated the British Government for Western education and Western science.[6]

As early as the Charter Act of 1813 it became a directive to the Governor General in Council to spend money for the introduction and promotion of a knowledge of the sciences among the inhabitant of British territories of India. Science education in India first started in the Calcutta Hindu College founded in 1817 under the leadership of Raja Ram Mohan Ray. But it must be noted that lack of equipments, lack of laboratories, inadequate teaching staff, shortage of funds and absence of any interest to develop the Indian economy through industrialization were some of the problem.[7]

After Independence India became intensively aware of the need of teaching science in a big way. Education Commission of 1948 recommended that 'as a part of general education for living, every step of education from primary school to the completion of undergraduate university work should include teaching of science. It is, however, recognised the need for different kinds of science courses for science and non-science students. The Commission felt that the aim of science course for the non-science students was not to make him a qualified scientist but to give him as much background as to make his general reading and experience in the field, interesting and intelligent. The course for science students was to be more rigorous, more in the nature of foundation for later specialization in the field.[8] Again the commission proposed two different types of science education for science and non science students.

The Education Commission of 1952 recommended that a 'general science' course with physics, chemistry and biology as the independent subject at the secondary school stage. It observed "It is to be noted that the science syllabus in the secondary school is not directed to the production of scientists. It aims is to give basic understanding and appreciation of scientific phenomena, biological and physical which may prepare the non-scientist for a fuller and more complete life. At the same time, the course should give fundamental principles to those relatively few who will later specialised in science."[9]

From the early years of freedom the nation realised that investment in science research and education was necessary to put the country on its facts, and to overcome the backwardness of the day of colonialism. The massive effort that was made during almost a quarter of a century has taken us a long way towards the realisation of her dream of India of the future. But to became truely self reliant, the nation will have to make a more determined effort to inculcate the spirit of self confidence among our people, and to generate the capacity to organise production according to the highest technological and scientific standards. In achieving the national objectives, the universities must play a vital role.[10]

The vestiges of colonialism will have to be taken off from

intellectual life. Our Universities should no longer look to the advance nations of the world for guidance in the matter of academic of technological developments, they will have to make for greater contribution to research and technology than they have made hitherto and they must establish for more intimate relations with the actual processes of production and problems of life than they have done so far. While the University must continue with the quest for knowledge for its own sake obviously this cannot be the only or even the primary principle guiding the research policy in our universities. Research and development have to be increasingly directed to the problems facing our society.[11]

It is the deep conviction of the Education Commission, that the progress, welfare and security of the nation depend critically on a rapid planned and sustained growth in the quality and extent of education and research in science and technology. Unfortunately our country is at the bottom of the G.N.P. per capita as also at the bottom of per capita expenditure of our research and education. However, in view of the limited resources the Commission has suggested some measures for the rapid growth of science education.[12]

The Commission feels that because of a rapid development of secondary and higher education and of research and industry, it is necessary that a several fold expansion in science education should take place. It is also necessary to develop a number of centres of advance study in science and mathematics. There staff should be of highest repute and should also have some members of international fame. UGC should make efforts to appoint some outstanding visiting professors. Some of our own eminent scientists working abroad should be invited. Besides these, the Commission has pointed out certain other measures such as removal of regional imbalances in development of science education, revision of the undergraduate and post-graduate curriculum, a proper balance between experimental and theoretical work, provision of well equipped workshops in every college and university department of science and encouraging the students to utilize these workshops more intensively, greater knowledge on the part of students of the theory of errors, basic statistical design and experiments, introducing flexibility and innovation in organising courses for the Masters degree closer relationship between science, technology and industry. Evening or correspondence courses for qualified industrial workers organising summer institute and production of the bulk of books in India by the end of the Fourth Plan and develop scientific technology etc.[13]

NATIONAL SCIENCE POLICY

(1) Science policy and decisions concerning science now play such a vital role in national economy and defence that it is most important for the governmental authorities at the highest level to ensure that on major scientific issues they can get advice which is as impartial and objective as it possibly can be. It is important to have an advisory body which is appropriate for this purpose. Besides heads of major agencies concerned with scientific research, persons who have a high standing and regard to their professions and who inspire general confidence a proportion of these members should be distinguished young scientists in their thirties. The number of such persons should not be less than the agency heads. They could be from the universities, research institutions (Government and non-government), industry and public life. The advisory body should also have on it not only scientists and technologists but also economists and social scientists and persons with experience of industry and management. The Scientific Advisory Committee to the Cabinet should be reorganised on the above lines and provided with an effective secretariat and with a professional component adequate to its tasks. The committee should be in a position to assess the broad scientific needs of the country including the universities and advise government of scientific policy and allocation of total resources between different sectors of scientific activities. It should also review continuously the national research policy situation.[14]

(2) It is our view that bodies concerned with science policy and implementation and which have executive and managerial functions requiring detailed and expert examination of diverse issues should ordinarily have professional scientists, engineers as science administrators of high standing as their chairman.[15]

(3) It should be a major task of the national research policy, and policies of the Universities to provide a climate conducive to research, and to prevent and eliminate, through energetic and public measures, all dangers and infringements of autonomy and freedom of action in research.[16]

(4) In determining our priorities for research, we should be guided by our own national needs and not be unduly influenced by what may happen to the current fashion in science.[17]

SCIENCE AND NATIONAL GOAL

The science policy resolution of 1958 of the Government of India illuminates clearly and concisely the relationship of science to national goals. And yet more than ten years later, most of us are largely dissatisfied with role that science is currently playing in promoting national goal.

Our national goals involve leap fagging from a state of economic backwardness and social disabilities attempting to achieve in a few decades a change which has historically taken centuries in other hands. This involves innovation at all levels. It was not until, and made responsible for the atomic energy programme of this country and came face to face with problem of development through the application of advanced technologies and basic research, that it became conscious of the problems that are encountered when the government has to perform a role which goes much beyond the maintenance of law and order and the security of the nation.[18]

SCIENCE ACADEMY

In the scientific life of a country a national organisation as academy of sciences occupy an exceedingly important role. In some way its role in crucial for the growth of science education and research. While this is not the place to go into the subject at any length.

In India the role of a National Academy is performed partly by the National Institute of Science. However, it may need some drastic re-organization, if the institute is to exercise a vigorous leadership in science and play a more significant role in the scientific activities of the nation. In recent decades the demarcation between science and technology has become increasingly thin and artificial, and for this and other reasons it may be desirable to widen the scope of the fellowship and bring into the Institute more engineers and technologists. Further, if the Institute is to be seriously concerned with the interaction between science, economic growth and national development, it would be useful to extend the fellowship to economists and social scientists. This is the practice in several academics, the most important being the Soviet Academy of Science.[19]

A National academy has also a major function in promoting international relation in science. Such a body represents the country on international scientific organizations such as the international Council of Scientific Unions and its various committees.

The Sixth Plan (Five Year Plan) 1980-85 document recognised the need of Science to the masses and emphasized. The task of creating a scientific temper is a vital necessity for growth of science and its utilization in the development process. There is need to create a scientific climate and to involve the people in discussions on various issues of science and technology which affects their life. There has to be dissemination of knowledge about natural phenomena and technological innovations through popular science journals and other media. There is also need for promoting public debate on major issue for eradication of the irrational attitudes which tend to hold back the nation from the path of progress.[20]

It is, therefore, essential that science and technology should be applied to find out new methods of utilising the various renewable energy sources. Such sources are solar energy, hydropower energy, biomass conversion, wind power, geothermal power etc. It is also necessary to develop the area of science and technology, for the development of Atomic Energy. Science ad technology for utilising Fast-breader Reactor and Fusion Technology have to be augmented, if the energy crisis is to be averted.[21]

The exploitation of marine resources has become necessary for the development of the country. New areas of science and technology has to be explored for exploitation of the oil at the sea bottom, sophisticated drilling ships fitted with computer and being used for drilling in the high seas. New methods of aerial survey have been developed for location of oil reserves. It has also been established that there are precious metals at the sea bottom and these can be recovered by utilising science and technology. Ocean Science has become a filed of competition for the nation to-day.[22]

The space science, although involves high expenditure and advanced expertise knowledge, it is indeed contributing in a big way to the development of the country. It is now possible to extend television facilities to remotest corner of our country through the geostationary satellite. It also helps the weather scientists to study and forecast weather more precisely. Space science also helps the ecologists to study the problem of maintaining ecological balance, by studying the overall changing pattern of forest cover in the landmass.[23]

Government of India recently started a new department of Bio-chemistry. This is because we feel that this is an area where India can reach tremendous heights, where we can be amongst the leaders. Bio-technology is used for agriculture, for health, for industry. The new advance on cellular and molecular biology must be used for finding practical solutions to many of our problems.[24]

The development of electronics and computer science have also occupied an important place in our country. Fast development of the science of electronics and computer, has brought in a big way the 'Robotic Revolution.' Robotics is a combination of expertise in a number of disciplines such as mechanical engineering, electronics and computer technology. It is estimated that by 1990 the international annual demand of robotic equipments may exceed five thousand crore of rupees. If India wants to get a share out of this scientific expertise should be developed from now. The Universities and other research institutes will have to play a big role in this.[25]

The recent discoveries which have led to the development of techniques of genetic engineering, cell fusion amongst plants, animals and micro-organisms, have so opened up new possibilities for the production of fuels from renewable resources, novel methods of crop fertilising and plant breeding, development of health care products from unconventional sources, new feed-stock, highly selective methods of pest control, waste treatment, pollution control and higher recoveries of petroleum and petro-chemicals. Bio-technology is essentially interdisciplinary in nature involving the most recent advances in the science of biology, chemistry, physics, mathematics and engineering.[26]

The developed countries possess the well advanced modern science, where as the underdeveloped do not. Modern science is necessary to India to get rid of poverty. It is definite that without modernising our methods of production we cannot produce enough to get rid of our poverty. Science can be used for destructive purposes; the same power can change the world for better. Only science alone can change India. There is no other way than to modernise India in methods of production. We have to absorb the spirit of science in India. We have applied the methods of science to our planning. There are bits of socialism in different Five Year Plan. Essentially it is not socialism but scientific planning in order to lay the base for greater progress in future.[27]

PROBLEMS OF SCIENCE EDUCATION

Science developed in every sense of the world but in every

step faces different critical situation. In modern times, science based technological education is providing successful in giving momentum to the process of economic development. Education helps to make the thinking, understanding and attitude of the citizen, comprehensive, wide, scientific objectives. Though it enables to solve the multitudinous problems, but our country still facing different problems. Some of them are discussed below :

Lack of Clear Objectives

In the existing system of science education both teachers and students are engaged in undergoing the formalities of the prescribed curriculum and are ignorant with regard to the aims and objectives of education. Aimless education is, generally, mechanical in nature and fails to give birth new ideas, originality and creativity. Though the recommendations and resolutions of various committees and commissions have time and again high-lighted the aims of education, no significant change is perceptible in the education.

Hence, clarity of national goal of science education in general and that of teaching objectives of a subject and lesson in particular is of paramount importance. The teachers and students approach to education should be objective standard.

Shortage of Institutions

Except standard colleges, the number of seats for science education are very few in number. Only the high meritorious students are admitted in the reputed colleges and most of the students of general merit are deprived of the science education. The science colleges are limited in number with a few seats and minimum facilities. Without proper institutional growth science education cannot progress in our society.

Unsuitable Curriculum and Text Books

As regard curriculum also no serious attempts have been made in the past to revise and reform it in the light of new changes. The curriculum of science education is of primitive nature and does not meet the modern requirements. It is mostly traditional and inappropriate in the changed conditions, and fails to direct and guide students into proper channels. There is also the problem of non-availability of suitable text books especially on science subjects. Language problem at this stage also adds to various other difficulties.

Unsuitable Laboratories

Laboratory is the part and parcel of science education. Every college possesses one laboratory for each department, but most of the colleges are in the name. Shortage of accommodation and different kind of apparatus create a big problem at the time of experiment. Without proper laboratory facility students can never progress in their education. Number of students in the class is more, but accommodation for them is not sufficient. Only in the old colleges apparatus and facilities are available, but all apparatus are old and students suffer a lot of grievances in these colleges also. Most of the colleges try to help students with facilities as many as they can.

Lack of Fund for Scientific Equipments

All scientific equipments are costly in price. Some of the colleges are not dim fit and proper to supply all the equipments due to shortage of money. Most of the equipments are smooth and small, when a new student handles it and lack of proper handling damages the equipments, but the college authority is not in a position to supply again in due time. For these drawbacks students suffer for the whole session. Most of the companies produced equipments of lower quality and supplied it in a low cost to the new colleges.

Inadequate Teaching Staff

In every kind of educational institution teachers' problem is one of the main problems. All the meritorious students attracted to the white colour job, like Engineer, Doctor, Veterinary Surgeon, Administrative job and Bank service etc. Nobody wants to go for teaching in their first choice, mainly in newly established colleges and in Higher Secondary Section teachers of science departments are always few in number. The function of laboratory and the classes is done by the demonstrator of the Department.

Absence of Interest

Problem of education is a day to day problem for present situation. College authority and the Government have no full attention for the economic side as well as experienced matter. But University Grants Commission gives sufficient stress for the development of science and technological education. Absence of interest for the science education hinders from its development and proper progress.

CONCLUSION

It can well be seen that science plays a big role in the development of the society in all aspects. We live in a world of fantastic scientific achievements. Science contributes to the maximum welfare and pleasure of man and also to the possibility of complete annihilation of mankind. It is important for every individual to know where he is and how he is to live there happily. Thus, science education is a crying need for mankind, considering the nature of science, its auto acceleration, two aspects of education and its aims of teaching in schools and colleges.

There is a greater demand for the incorporation of science into every part of the society by drawing all the resources available in the community. Science for the masses should be viewed as the contribution to the development, dissemination and application of scientific and technical know how, in the development of the individual and country as a whole.

As a result of the present investigation we can assess that due to limited seats in the science departments of the Universities many science graduates were refused for admission during the last few years. This problem may be solved by expanding seats in the various science departments of the Universities. And science education must spread to the rural areas in a big way and people must be involved more meaningfully.

NOTES

1. Kothari, D.S., *Kothari Commission Report*, 1964-66, NCERT, 1971, p. 719.
2. *Ibid.*, p. 718.
3. Das, R.C., (Publication of Paper), *Teaching of Science is Secondary Stage*, Symposium 1973, GUTA, p. 57.
4. Bajalee College Silver Jubilee 1980-81, 25th December — *Science and Technological Education and Development of Human Resources Perspective to Eighties*, Report of the Seminar.
5. Gandhi, I., Children's Day Prime Minister Lecture 12 October, 1981, Ministry of Information and Broadcasting, Delhi.
6. Rawat, P.L., *History of Indian Education*, 1985, Ram Prasad and Sons, Agra-3, p. 153.
7. Biswas and Agarwal, *Indian Education Documents since Independence*, Sterling Publishers Private Limited, 1971, p. 403.
8. *Ibid.*, p. 404.
9. Hassan, N., *Challenges in Education, Cultures and Social Welfare*, Allied Publishers Pvt. Limited, New Delhi, 1976, p. 57.
10. *Ibid.*, 1976, p. 57.
11. *Ibid.*, p. 58.
12. Rawat, P.L., *History of Indian Education*, Ram Prasad and sons, Agra-3, 1985, p. 400.
13. *Ibid.*, p. 401.
14. Kothari, D.S., *Report of the Education Commission* 1964-66, NCERT, Delhi, 1971, p. 764.
15. *Ibid.*, p. 765.
16. *Ibid.*, p. 766.
17. *Ibid.*, p. 766.
18. Saravai, V., *Science Policy and National Development*, Macmillan, Delhi, 1974, p. 3.
19. Kothari, D.S., *Kothari Commission*, 1964-66, NCERT, Delhi, 1971, p. 767.
20. A.I.U., *University News*, Vol. XXIV, N-7, May 1/86, p. 5.
21. Gandhi, R., *Social Benefit Main Trust of Scientific Research*, Address of Prime Minister at the Om Prakash Bhasin Award for Science and Technology, 17th March, 1986, New Delhi.

22. *Ibid.*
23. *Ibid.*
24. *Ibid.*
25. *Ibid.*
26. *Ibid.*
27. Phukan, P.D.C., *Ideas Shaking The World*, 1973, p. 66.

5

University Education

INTRODUCTION

Universities may be called as the home of learning. Its standard and efficiency of teaching regarding the higher knowledge depends upon the mental and moral acquisition of the society. No doubt Universities are the only seats of higher knowledge from where the society can get the leaders in science, arts and various other fields of national life. A University must never forget its obligations to the society. The prosperity of the country is linked with university. The University is the place where the fate of the nation is moulded and shaped. Its success is judged by the type of young men and women it produces and the volumes of researches it makes. A University is an institution consciously developed to the pursuit of knowledge, the solution of problems, the critical appreciation of achievement and the training of men at a really high level. It is nothing but a community of scholars and students engaged in the task of seeking truth. These things are required of a University, professional training, education of the whole man and research for a University is simultaneously a professional school, cultural centre and a research institution. We can mention here the opinion of Late Pandit Jawaharlal Nehru. According to him, "University stands for humanism, for tolerance, for reason, for adventure of ideas and for the search of truth. It stands for onward march of the human race towards higher objectives. If the University discharges its duties adequately, then it is well with the nation and the people."

Again Dr. S.Radhakrishnan says, "The University should be the inspiring home of all the sciences as well as the preparation gramed for civic life. Its departments should be not only co-existent but co-operative. They all have to work in close harmony."[1]

AIMS AND OBJECTIVES OF UNIVERSITY EDUCATION

Dr. Radhakrishnan, an eminent educationist who chaired the University Education Commission of 1948 made the following recommendations regarding the aims and objects of Indian Universities. They are :

(1) Universities are the organs of civilization.

(2) Universities are the institutions of intellectual adventure.

(3) It is the institutions of an integrated way of life.

(4) Universities develop the wisdom and knowledge.

(5) Aims of social order develop in the universities.

(6) Universities develop the love for higher values of life.

(7) It is the field of adjustment of society and new changes.

(8) It is the Institutions for training for leadership.

(9) Universities are the main centre of cultural unity.

(10) Universities are the centre of critical study of the past.

(11) Universities develop the world, mindedness and national sentiment.[2]

FUNCTIONS OF UNIVERSITIES

With the aims of university there are some functions of University which are related in the proper development. Kothari Commission 1964 discussed the following functions of Universities :

(1) to seek and cultivate new knowledge, to engage vigorously and fearlessly in the pursuit of truth, and

to interpret old knowledge and beliefs in the light of new needs and discoveries.

(2) to provide right kind of leadership in all walks of life, to identify gifted youth and help them their potential to the full by cultivating physical fitness, developing the powers of the mind and cultivating right interests, attitudes and moral and intellectual values.

(3) to provide society with competent men and women trained in agriculture, arts, medicine, science and technology and various other professions, who will also be cultivated individuals, imbued with a sense of social purpose.

(4) to strive to promote equality and social justice and to reduce social and cultural differences through diffusion of education.

(5) to foster in the teachers and students, and through them in society generally, the attitudes and values needed for developing the "good" life in individuals and society.[3]

HISTORICAL BACKGROUND

University education is not a new system for our country. In ancient time the universities occupied an important place in our country. From the very ancient time tradition of learning which corresponds to the colleges of modern times. There were 'Gurukulas' and 'Ashrams' run by individual scholars in ancient times. Students approached to these institutions for the recognition of their merits. The earliest University was 'Takshashilla' which attained a great fame as the University of seventh century B.C.[4]

During the Buddhist Period, a number of 'Viharas' and 'Sangharams' or monasteries developed in to a kind of educational centre. The Universities of Purushapura (Peswar), Takshashilla (west Punjab), Jaggaddal, Vikramshila and Odantapuri (Madras), Vallabhi (Saurastra) were the prominent centres of higher education. These richly endowed institutions were attributed by the students from different places. Many of the students had an international reputation. The teachings were fairly comprehensive and included ritual and holy scriptures, grammar and astronomy, medicine, logic and the different systems of philosophy.[5]

During the British Period, 'the Woods Despatch' of 1854 was a landmark, as it had recommended establishing of Universities of modern type of India. As a result of the recommendations of the 'woods Despatch' modern University education in India began in 1857 when the Universities of Calcutta, Bombay and Madras were founded by the British. A fourth university in Allahabad was set up in 1887. But prior to the establishment of those universities, India had organised a long tradition of Higher knowledge which covered that subjects like theology, indigenous medicine, sanskrit and arabic literature, astronomy, mathematics, grammer, rhetoric, law and the likes. Importance was given to the old subjects as a result of which modern science could not thrive. But on the other hand, it originated modern education movement. It will be interesting to note that the first three universities, established in India, patterned largely after the earlier model of London University and paradoxically by that time London University was itself abondoning that model.[6]

The next landmark, in the University education that attracts our attention, is the appointment of the Indian University Commission of 1902 during the viceroyalty of Lord Curzon. His contribution to the development of Higher education, was unique and praiseworthy. This Commission and the Indian Universities Act of 1904 aimed at strengthening and reconstituting of the entire system of the universities of the country. The Government of India, resolution of 1913, also helped the reconstitution of the Universities whenever necessary, The Calcutta University Commission of 1917 too was another milestone in the history of University education in India. Other important milestones in the field, were the establishment of

Inter University Board in 1924 and the Hartog Committee Report of 1929 in the pre-Independence era.[7]

As the years passed away, India got its Independence and the mode of the Universities began to change. New Universities sprang up in different places and India came to possess 227 (193+34) Universities teaching and affiliating type with a medium of teaching wings.[8]

Today India has had the third position in the world in number of the Universities, she is possessing and the standard she is maintaining. India is now next to the USA and USSR in this system.

In the middle of the present century, there were 12 universities in England, 4 in Scotland and one in Wales, With 4 associated colleges, and one in Ireland. By the beginning of the nineteenth century there established only 2 famous Universities — Oxford and Cambridge. These two universities are the oldest universities in England. Later on Darban University was opened in 1832 and London University in 1836. During later half of the 19th century other Universities also were established. Some of them were University colleges associated with universities at the beginning and got the full status of the University at the inception of the twentieth century. It may be noted hat the number of Universities in Great Britain increased along with the increase of population.[9]

In the beginning, the nature of Higher Education in the USA was like that of Europe. Both the educational systems were dominated by specialization and research methods. But the American philosophy of life changed with the needs of the time and so the aim of Higher education also changed. Consequently, a vast difference in the nature of European and American education now exists. Higher education being specialised and research oriented was neither accessible to all, nor public. University education connected with specialization and research was useful for brilliant students only. Average students were neglected for higher education. In the year 1975 in America the number of universities rose to about 200 and that of colleges of

Higher education to about 2000. The number of students in liberal Arts college increased to 80,00,000. Now there are two kinds of universities in the USA — Private Universities and State Universities.[10]

PROBLEMS OF UNIVERSITY EDUCATION

After Independence, many of the universities in our country are getting a low estimation in the eyc of public. In spite of several commissions and committees set up since the Independence and headed by the educational experts, the sad and deplorable state of affairs in the field of higher education is still persisting. The standard of education imparted, the attitude of the teachers and the students have all made the university education a fiasco.

The explosion of knowledge has given a rise to noticeable tendencies. In the last 40 years the teaching departments of the universities have grown considerably to a large extent and they have better resources to maintain in the better standard and function mainly at the post-Graduate and Research levels. In spite of this expansion, however, the colleges are still having a dominant position in the provision of the facilities for higher education.

The falling standard of education in various universities at present is causing a great anxiety. The administration, educationists and other concerned with education are making effort to check this evil by commissions and conferences of Vice Chancellors. They have thrown light on the causes of this deteriorating in standard. According to many surveys the main cause of this evil is the lack of interest shown by the teachers in teaching. These days teachers have to take more classes. Manpower of doing work has a limit and teachers can only prepare themselves for teaching to a certain extent. As such by increasing the working hours of the number of classes the standard of teaching naturally goes down.

As a result of the evaluation of the problems of Higher

Education it is, investigated that the following factors are responsible for the deterioration of Higher Education.

Aimlessness

To-day by and large, students in higher educational institutions suffer from the problem of aimlessness. They are not clear about aims of education in life. Aimless education gives birth to a frustration and disillusionment. Most of the students suffer from this disease. They manage to pass various examinations without any clearcut goal in view. This leads to a great harm. One should be very clear about the aim of pursuing a particular course of study. This needs availability of proper guidance in services.

Problem of Expansion

As the population is increasing day by day, educational facilities are also expanding. The implementation of various plans is leading to the establishment of a large number of colleges and universities. But due to economic constraints, it is well nigh impossible to provide higher education to each and every child. The facilities available in our country are few and far between. There is no denying the fact, that every child wishes to get higher education. Therefore, some checks will have to applied. Our prime duty is to provide with the higher institutions first to those students who are talented and meritorious. Apart from this, in a democracy there is need to encourage the poor, backward, schedule castes, schedule tribes, minorities and girls etc. on the basis of equality. They are to be provided with the facilities of scholarships, freeships and book aids etc. in adequate number. Other facilities like laboratory, library, hostel and playground etc. are also to be increased considerably.

Problem of Admissions

Higher education is a very costly affair. Due to the indigent economic condition of the country, it is not possible to provide higher education to all. Though the number of higher educational institutions as well as the enrollment has increased considerably in recent years yet they have not been able to keep pace with the every growing demand for higher education. Under the prevailing situation the admission policy should be re-organised and standardised.

Problem of Curriculum

Present curriculum of the University Education also suffers from many deficiencies and defects. It is generally, theoretical, heavy subject centred and fails to meet the needs of life and aspirations of the people. It lacks integration between general and vocational education. In modern times, curriculum needs to be related to the life and should be experienced centred. Emphasis should be laid on its practical and functional aspects.

Problem of Teachers

The present condition of the University teachers is not satisfactory. A teacher must be acceptable to the students in respect to his behaviour, his mastery over the subject, his philosophy, attitude and so on. But at present most of teachers serving in different colleges and university have neither ability nor aptitude for the profession and they teach mechanically and listlessly. A large proportion of teachers suffers from financial hardship and they are unable to buy books and journals which are required for their profession. Physical facilities in some of the colleges are not so conductive to effective teaching.

Methods of Teaching

The lecturing methods of teaching is much in vogue in higher education. In this system, students become passive listeners. The education thus imported is informative and mechanical. It does not go deep to the understanding and reflective levels. There is need to make students active participants in the teaching-learning process. This is necessary for proper interaction. Teachers should take help of other dynamic methods of teaching like question answer, supervised study, discussions and seminars etc. This will help to develop the students thinking, arguing and imagining powers.

Medium of Education

Medium of instruction creates a controversial problem in our university education. In college level particularly for undergraduate education the medium of instruction is regional language, but on the other hand, in post-Graduate level the medium of instruction is English. It is true that through the medium of mother tongue students are able to express themselves better, but in the transitional period, there is a dearth of original works of high order in regional language, and will take time to stabilise. In post-Graduate level students has suffered a lot and fallen in awkward position.

Problem of Examination

The present system of examination is defective. Defective system of examination is bound to affect the standard of both teaching and learning. The prevailing system of examination lays undue emphasis on eliciting factual information and the teaching learning process gears to the acquisition of such information by the students. The whole system of examination is not only invalid, unreliable and inadequate but also tends to corrupt the moral students of University life. So adequate step should be taken to bring about desirable modifications and a new approach should be devised in the system of examination.

Poor Research Work

One of the chief aims of higher education is to search for truth. This requires conducting research works of a high order. It should be an original contribution to the fund of knowledge. But unfortunately, research is suffering both in standard and quality. The system has given birth to evil practices and in an attack on our moral character. Teachers' community cannot disown this responsibility. The tone is to be set by them. Rules and regulations in this regard should be strictly followed. Research should be an honest, hard and dedicated work leading to original contribution.

Economic Problem

Economic problem is one of the major problems of higher education. Proper maintenance of libraries, laboratories, hostels and playgrounds etc. involve a huge cost. Quality and standards demand more facilities. Education had been a state subject and state government always shows its inability to manage the affairs properly. It thinks that education is a factor of consumption and make things difficult. This attitude should undergo a radical change. A liberal policy should be adopted in this respect. It is the duty of the Central, State and Local Self Government etc., to place adequate funds at the disposal of educational institutions and to help them in all possible ways.

Students Unrest

In University and Colleges the problem of indiscipline is a grave one. Party politics among the students community makes the situation worst. Majority of the students come from comparatively or entirely from rural homes having no genuine interest or ability for higher education. It is rather disheartening to note that a sizeable portion of the student population goes to college just to pass time and take little interest in studies when once admitted. Some people hold that arts students are responsible for indiscipline in educational institutions for their dark futures. Wide spread mass uses to copy and make unfairmeans in examinations which clearly indicate the motive of the students in pursuing studies. As if, to obtain degree is the main aim and object of their study.

Lack of Freedom

Autonomy should be the main criteria of educational institutions. But the position is in the reverse order. Due to financial constraints political parties and government put obstructions and interfere in their working. This gives rise to evil practices. Generally, appointments of higher posts are politically motivated. Institutions should be free to create academic atmosphere. Merits alone should be the basis for filling up the teaching posts. Autonomy of the University, Colleges and departments should be uphold at all costs. Teachers and students should be free in academic matters.

Problem of Administration

Another burning problem of Higher Education is the problem of administration. In the day to day life of the educational institutions have to face a larger number of problems and the administration has to grapple with them. These sometimes take a violent turn and result in strikes, sitting and misbehaviour with the authorities. It may be due to party politics among the teachers, and students and the management involving outside elements. The administration is to be vigilant in this respect. It should proceed democratically but firmly.

CONCLUSION

University is an important institution that is concisely devoted to the pursuit of knowledge, the solution of problems, the critical appreciation of achievement and the training of men at a really high level. Our Universities have to face a lot of difficulties from time to time with regard to their autonomy and persons in power interfere in their internal matters. In fact, many of the seeming obstacles are due primarily to the fact that our universities have been exotic and have not grown from the soil. Here we can mention the idea of *Cardinal Newman* that "A University training aims at raising the intellectual tone of society, at cultivating the public mind, at purifying the national taste, at supplying true principles to popular enthusiasm and fixed aims to popular aspiration, at giving enlargement and sobriety to the idea of the age, at facilitating the exercise of political power and refining the intercourse of private life."[11]

NOTES

1. Radhakrishnan, S., Convocation Address 1951, 1st Convocation, Gauhati University.
2. Radhakrishnan, S., University Education Commission 1948-49, Government of India.
3. Kothari, D.S., *Report of the Education Commission*, 1964-66, NCERT, 1971, pp. 497-98.

4. Lulla and Murty, *Essential Problems of Indian Education*, L.N. Agarwal, Educational Publishers, Agra-3, 1971, p. 40.
5. Mukerjee, S.N., *Education in India Today and Tomorrow*, Vadodara 1971, p. 167.
6. Mathur, M.V., Ruhela, S.P., *Tasks of Universities in India*, Kalyani Publishers, 1976, p. 1.
7. Mukerjee, S.N., *Education in India Today and Tomorrow*, Acharya Book Depot, Vododara, 1976, p. 167.
8. University News, April II, 1998.
9. Chaube, S.P., Comperative Education System, Prakashan Kendra, Lucknow, 1992, p. 10.
10. *Ibid.*
11. Newman, C., *Idea of a University*.

6

Local Authority and Higher Education

INTRODUCTION

Local authority is a contrivance by which the People of the locality are made to participate more closely in some of the functions of the state particularly bearing upon the local areas. It implies a devolution of functions which is necessary corollary of the democratic government. Thus, Gilchrist says "the term localself government is applied to those organs which exist at the will of the Central Government and which, while they exist, have certain definite powers of making regulation, of controlling certain parts of public finance and of executing their own laws, or the laws of the central legislature over a given area. These organs are essentially subordinate bodies, but they have independence of action within stated limits. They represent a subdivision of functions of governments, for the purpose of efficient adminstration''.[1]

Localself Government is that part of the State Government in federal countries dealing mainly with local affairs, administered by authorities subordinate of the state Government. The local authority may be elected and partly nominated or wholly nominated members. Normally the State Government has no Jurisdiction within the local area in respect of matters administered by the local authority. Local authorities are the creation of the state legislature. It has substantial autonomy, considerable fiscal and administrative independence. Local government's work is amateur. Its work is largely personal. Local authorities are of two kinds, local and quasi local. The first is territorial and older. The second is functional created for the administration of special purposes.[2]

Government is the agency through which the will of the state is expressed. We cannot think of state without Government. It is a vehicle of the state. The government conducts and regulates the affairs of the state and promotes the social, economic and political welfare of the state. A people settled in a definite territory cannot constitute a state till some organization has been formed. Government is the organization which establishes the essential relation of command and obedience. Government exists wherever that is confirmed, whether it is a vast organization like that of the United States, or in simple tribal government of the Austrian aborigines.[3]

It is the focus of the common purpose of the people. Government is the outward manifestation of the State, and as such is the organization of the common purposes of the people.

The Directive Principles of State Policy (Article 40) said "The State shall take steps to organise village Panchayats and endow then with such powers and authority as may be necessary to enable them to function as units of self Government."

The village Panchayats have been the oldest administrative units in India. Panchayats are much more than units of Localself Government. They are essentially the agencies of rural development 'Gram Sabha' constitute a loboratory of village democracy. Panchayat samities occupy central place in the three tier structure of Panchayati Raj.

Municipal Boards is the administrative body of the urban area. At the beginning, the Municipal Boards were held responsible for repairing, cleaning, lighting or watching any public streets, roads, drains, tanksets. But in some cases the boards were authorised to undertake other works of public utility which were calculated to promote the health, comfort and convenience of the inhabitants. At present the Municipalities are entrusted with wide variety of functions.

District Councils are some other administrative bodies for the Hills' areas. They are empowered to establish and manage primary schools, dispensaries, markets, cattle pound to maintain roads and waterways. The District councils have legislative, executive and judicial powers under the provision of the Sixth schedule to the Constitution.

ROLE OF LOCAL AUTHORITY

Local authority and the government played an important role in the development and expansion of Higher education. In the present century people established colleges, collect fund for the financial security and elect one preparation committee. After the preparation, students are admitted and form a college Governing Body. After the completion of all requisite qualifications the university affiliated the institutions and bring under the control of university and sends the report to the Government. After some years, if the Government is satisfied the college comes under ad-hoc or recurring grant for the development and bring under deficit system of grants-in-Aid.

In the post-Independence period the policy of grant-in-aid becomes more vigorous. The government and private agencies have been working together in close co-operation. Private agencies have played a predominant role in all fields of education and at all stages from the primary to the University all over the country and have been specially active in the field of higher education. There has been a very large expansion both in the number of institutions and students.

The administration and control of higher education in our country is dual responsibility of both the government and the University. However, to look after the day to day administration of the colleges (both Government and Non-Government) there is a Governing body for each college, consisting of teachers, Government nominees, educationists and representatives from the parents and local social workers. But in both the colleges the academic side such as prescribing the courses of studies. and qualification of teachers, holding of examination, requirement of laboratories, libraries equipments etc., are under the control of University. Regarding selection of teachers in the Government colleges they are appointed by the Selection committee. The Universities are autonomous bodies. They are managed by the Court, Executive Council, Academic Council etc.

The recommendations of the kher Committee were not universally adopted by all the states. We find that there is no uniform pattern of administration. Even after the re-organisation of the states in 1956, in some parts of the country education is administered for the State Governments. While in others responsibility for primary education has been entrusted to local bodies. In some states municipalities run Secondary Schools and College also.[4]

But in the USSR, the local unit played an important role. Districts, cities and towns form other independent units in the Soviet education system. The District is the largest unit which sub-divided into cities and towns which have their own department of education. Many rural regions have combined to form a rural education district is given legislative, administrative and executive powers. But truely speaking, these powers are used by the local Executive Committee which is formed by the Soviet Union according to the direction of communist party.[5]

On the other hand, there are about 129 Local Education Authorities for the province of England and about 17 for wales. Under these 146 local Education Authorities there are 62 Administrative Committees, 83 County Boroughs and a joint board of representatives makes 146 Local Education Authorities. The Administrative Committees are of different sizes depending upon the population and financial resources of the areas concerned. For example, the area of London Council is about 303 square kilometres and that of Lancashire County Council is about 5200 sq. k.m. County Borough and County Council are under the Local Education Authority.

Educational organisation in the USA is in the hands of local

Education Board. County Board system are mainly found in villages.[6]

ROLE OF GOVERNING BODY

Under the order of the Government of 5th April, 1905 it was decided that no college or High school would be affiliated to the University unless it was placed under the management of a regularly constituted Governing Body (GB) or a Committee.[7]

(1) Every Government aided college shall be governed by a Governing Body, the constitution of which has been approved by the Director of Public Instruction, save in cases where the secretary to the Government of Education Department allows an exception under special circumstances.

The Governing Body shall consist of the following members namely :

1. Principal — Ex-officio
2. Vice-Principal — Ex-officio
3. Two representatives of the teaching staff to be elected annually by the teachers from among themselves.
4. The Inspector of the Schools of the circle as an educationist nominated by the state govt.
5. Two persons nominated by the University.
6. Two persons to be nominated by the State Government.
7. Donors nominee : Donors paying Rs. 25,000.00 or more or their nominees not more than one person being nominated by each donor to be life members.

8.(a) The persons other than the members of the teaching staff to be co-oped by the other members, at least one of whom shall be a guardian and another shall be a lady.

(b) The President shall be nominated by the State Government.

(c) The Secretary shall be nominated by Government

and if the Principal is not nominated, he shall be the Joint Secretary.

(2) Seven members present shall form a quorum.

(3) The Governing Body shall meet at least once a quarter.

(4) The college shall satisfy the University, that it is under the management of a regularly constiuted Governing Body on which the teaching staff is adequately represented.

(5) The proceedings of the Governing Body's meeting shall be sent to the Director of Public Instruction and the concerned University and no final decision regarding appointment, promotion and dismissal of the members of the teaching staff including the Principal or construction involving Rs. 5000/- or more shall be taken without prior approval of the Director of Public Instruction.

(6) On the recommendation of the Director of Public Instruction, the State Government may, if satisfied after due notice and enquiry, order reconstitution of Governing Body and pending its reconstitution, the Director of Public Instruction, may take over the control and management of the college.

(7) No act or proceeding of the Governing Body shall be invalidated merely by reason of any vacancy in its membership.

(8) Unless on an emergency the meetings of the Governing Body shall be held in the college premises and the records of the meeting shall be regularly kept and be opened to inspection by the Director of Public Instruction and the concerned University.

(9) The tenure of Governing Body shall be ordinarily for 3 years from the date of formation. The Director of Public Instruction may extend the term pending reconstitution of the Governing Body.

(10) The following particular duties are assigned to the Governing Body :

(a) To undertake the financial management of the college, to collect authorised subscriptions, to see that the fees are realised and that exemption from payment for fees are not granted except in accordance with the rules in force.

(b) To arrange for maintenance of the college building, furniture and equipment required.

(c) To grant leave for the teachers subject to the prescribed rules. The grant of leave other than casual leaves, and the arrangement made to fill the vacancy being reported to the D.P.I. and concerned University.

(d) To appoint persons in connection with the affairs of the college.

(e) To arrange for half yearly internal audit for the all college funds and verification of stock and furniture. These duties shall ordinarily be entrusted to one or two members of the Governing Body, other than the office bearer and teacher members. If there is no such members in the body competent to take up these duties the body may employ an outsider for the purpose on reasonable payment if funds permit.

(11) Except where it is ordered otherwise by general for special orders, the Governing Body will leave to the principal all routine matters in connection with arrangement of classes, admission and transfer of pupils, settlement of class routine, periodical examination, awarding of class promotion and all matter of routine relating to instruction, administration and discipline and control of pupils and the staff. In case of any complaint, it will be open to the Governing Body, however, to depute one or more of their members to make an enquiry into any of these matters if necessary, and to report there to the Governing Body and will forward a copy of the report to the Director of Public Instruction and the concerned University.

(12) The other duties and functions of the Governing Body are as follows :

(i) To determine the general scheme of studies of the college subject to the approval by the concerned

University and to obtain the approval of the State Government through the DPI with regard to the inclusion of additional subjects and creation of new post.

(ii) To consider and initiate projects for the improvement of the college.

(iii) To deal with questions of

  (a) Discipline and

  (b) Grant of fee remission under rules prescribed by the State Government.

(iv) To deal with any question and exercise any function that may be referred to or assigned by the State Government or the concerned University.

Role of Government

The role of the Central Government in Education is limited to providing leadership, helping the states and private bodies in expanding and improving education, including higher education, maintaining standard of Higher education, research, scientific and technical education, administering, expanding and improving education in the Union territories and preservation of National culture.

The State Government started as units of educational administration with the appointment of Director of Public Instruction and Inspectors to assist them. They mainly deal with recognition and inspection of school and colleges and recommending grants-in-aid. However, the policy continued to be centralised, with Mentford reforms education was transferred to the States in 1921. The JES was abolished. Education was put under the charge of elected ministers responsible to the State Legislature.[8]

After Independence the Indian Constitution made the states responsible for education all stages with certain exception, such as the Central Universities at Benaras, Aligarh, Delhi and

Santiniketon, institution for scientific and technical education financed by the Central Government, institutions for scientific research and technology etc. Thus, education at all stages is a state responsibility of co-ordination and maintenance of standard of higher levels in the centre.[9]

Article 45 of the Constitution directs the states "to endevour to provide, within a period of ten years from the commencement of Constitution for free and compulsory education for all children untill they complete the age of fourteen years''.

In recent years there is growing rapidly a trend of close co-operation between the centre and states. The centre is in a position to give more and more financial help and so it secure their co-operation by appointment of a number of central councils and committees, such as the Central Advisory Board, the All India Council of Secondary Education, the National Council of Education Research and Training. Besides these bodies there are representatives of the states and the centre and also some well-known educationists, co- operation is also secured by exchanging views through seminars and conferences. However, in present pattern the initiative for education and educational reform and re-organisation lies with the states.[10]

The machinery for educational administration in the state is composed of the Department of Education headed by a Minister, who is responsible to the legislature and is appointed by the Chief Minister. In some states he is assisted by Deputy Minister. The Minister exercises his authority through the officers of the Department and other agencies, like the Universities, Statutory Boards etc. and is assisted by the Education Secretary at the Secretariate level and the Director of Education, who is the Chief Executive Officer of the Department.

Education Minister

Education Secretary

State University

Director of Education and Joint Director

Education Committee

Deputy Director

Statutory Board of Education

Functions of Education Department

(1) Framing of policies, proceedings, rules, regulation and determining standards.

(2) Inspection and evaluation to determine efficiency of operation.

(3) To run schools and colleges established by government and to control private institutions.

(4) To deal with matters regarding curricula and text books.

(5) To co-ordinate educational programmes of the state in order to promote efficiency.

(6) To provide leadership for planning and research.

(7) To provide consultative and information services.

The minister is, generally, a non-technical man with almost little experience of either education or administration. He has to learn heavily on the bureaucracy for guidance. He can make or mar the whole education system. 'If he is a man of vision, courage and devotion, he can provide the leadership for the development of an educational program in his state which will meet the needs of the individual and of society. On the other hand, if he is lacking in vision, courage and administrative ability, the education of the state cannot be progressive.'[11]

Education Secretary or Commissioner frames policies and

passes orders on behalf of the Government. He is generally a man from the I.A.S. He acts as a link between the Minister and Director. The Director's proposals are critically examined by the staff of the Secretariat before being submitted for the approval of the Minister.

DIRECTORATE OF EDUCATION

Directorate of education is an executive body carrying out the policies of the government. Its main functions are :

(1) To present proposals of policy to the Secretary and to execute them as approved by the Minister.

(2) To supervise, control, inspect and guide all educational institutions in the State.

(3) To keep government informed about the conditions and progress of all types of education and the people's need and requirement regarding education.

(4) To disburse fund as sanctioned by the Government.

(5) To provide expert advise both to the institution and secretariate.

Director of Education

Director of education is the highest officer of the Directorate of Education. Recently the Directorate of Education is divided into five separate section, such as Higher Education, Secondary Education, Elementary Education, Technical Education and Social Education. In some states a Director has been appointed from the administrative services, but generally he is a technical expert and chosen for long teaching, inspecting and administrative experience in the department. As the highest executive, he is responsible for the administration of education in the entire state. Assisted by a number of deputy and assistant Directors he performs the following duties :

(1) To supervise the work of the government officials, inspectors, teachers of the government institutions and to deal with their leave, transfer and discipline.

(2) To determine disburse the grants-in-aid to the state, Universities, local bodies and the large number of privately managed institutions.

(3) To supervise, control, inspect and guide the private institutions.

(4) To act as Chairman of the State Board of Secondary Education and examining body and to administer and exercise emergency powers in this respect. Some Boards of Secondary Education have a whole time Chairman who is not the Director.

(5) To act a member of the syndycate, executive council of the state University.

(6) To frame policies and proposals and submit them to the secretary for the approval of the Minister.

(7) To administer education throughout the state.

(8) To organise the training of primary and secondary teachers where this is not done by the University.

ROLE OF UNIVERSITY GRANTS COMMISSION

With the recommendation of the University Education Commission, a University Grants Commission was established in November 1953 by a resolution of the Ministry of Education for the purpose of allocation and disbursement of Grants to Universities as well as for the purpose of co-ordination and maintenance of standards of education in India. The powers and functions of the Commission were enlarged in January 1954. The constituent colleges of the university of Delhi were brought within the purview of the Commission in April 1955. The commission has since been accorded statutory recognition with effect from November 5, 1956 under the University Grants Commission Act, 1956 as passed by the Parliament, with effect from the date the commission has been reconstituted with a chairman and eight other members.[12]

For the purpose and the development grants to both Central and State Universities, the commission asks each University to prepare and send to the commission a detail statement of the proposals it has improvements, expansion and development of teaching and research over a period of five years corresponding to the Five Year Plan periods of the Government of India. These statements are scrutinised by a special committee composed of a few well-known persons representing various field of learning, drawn from the universities and outside. The proposals are examined by the Commission and a visiting committee. The visiting committee visits on the spot of the development programme of a University, and on this basis the commission makes the grant. In the field of engineering and technology the commission generally acts on the advice of the All India Council for Technical Education.

Thus, we find that the University Grants Commission has been empowered with extensive powers to finance and develop higher education keeping in tune with the national requirements. The commission has been spending money for purposes of developing university education since its establishment. This money has been paid towards the development of humanities as well as advancement of higher scientific education, research engineering education and technology.

CONCLUSION

Local authorities in our country were the creation of Lord Ripon's reforms and these were entrusted with the care of primary education on the same basis as the school boards did in England after 1870. But the difference lays in the fact that while the local authority in India were created by an executive order, the boards in Britain were created by legislature. Lack of legislation was the most striking trait in the Indian system. This deficiency caused lack of the required alertness, initiative and sincere efforts on the part of the local authority. In England a series of Acts were passed designed to make compulsory education a real success. A similar effort in India would have been highly conducive to the cause of expansion of general education.

Our present study shows that local public constitute preparation committee and started educational institutions for the development of higher education. In some cases particularly the technical and professional institutions are established by the Government directly. Governing Body is one of the important local bodies for the development of Higher Education. Under the order of the government of April 5, 1905 it was decided that no college or High School would be affiliated to the university unless it was placed under the management of a regularly constituted governing body or a committee.

The Central and the State Government in education is limited to providing leadership helping the states and private bodies in expanding and improving education, including higher education, maintaining standard of higher education, research, scientific and technical education.

We find that the University Grants Commission has been empowered with extensive powers to finance and develop higher education keeping in tune with the national requirments, thus fulfilling the most urgent need for the establishment of a body to take up these functions. The UGC has a role in the promotion of high quality of research mainly applied research, in the removal of regional imbalances in the development of higher education and in the promotion of values in the academic community so that its commitment to the pursuit of truth and excellence is enhanced and it is able to discharge its responsibilities more efficiently and effectively.

NOTES

1. Jinker, H., *Foundation of Local Self Government in India, Pakistan and Burma*, Lalvani Publishing House, Bombay.
2. Rao, V.K. Hazarika, N., *Local Self Government in India*, S. Chand and Company, Ram Nagar, New Delhi, 55, 1985, p. 10
3. Gilchrist, R. N., *Principle of Political Science*, Orient Longman, Madras. 2, pp. 29-30.
4. Bhatnagar, Verma, *Educational Administration*, Loyal Book Depot., Delhi, 1981, p. 160.
5. Hans, N., *Comparative Education*, Orient Longman, London, 1971, p. 139

6. Chaube, S.P., *Comperative Education System*, Prakashan Kendra, Lucknow, 1982, p. 74.
7. Govt. of Assam, *Report on the province of Assam and Bengal* 1910-11, Vol., p. 39.
8. Bhatnagar and Verma, *Educational Administration*, Loyal Book Depot, Delhi, 1981, p. 142.
9. *Ibid.*, p. 153.
10. *Ibid.*, p. 153.
11. *Ibid.*, p. 155.
12. U.G.C. Act, 1956, Section 12, As provided.

7

Problems of Education in Rural Areas

INTRODUCTION

India is not a country of urban areas. It is full of innumerable villages. Most of the population of the country lives in the villages. According to 1991 census 76.17 percent population lives in 5.75 lacs of villages. Nearly 4.50 lacs of villages have a population of less than 1,000 persons. There are hardly, 1,000 villages with optional population size of 10,000.[1]

This makes it obvious that any process of planning and development in India can hardly succeed without transforming its 'Rural Society'. The destiny of great India is reshaped through planned development. This great programme of national development, involves a colosal task of reconstruction of lacs of villages. The villages are remaining backward due to poverty, ignorance and disease, repression, exploitation and negligence through ages. The villages should be made prosporous, interesting and culturally rich to live in. This great task of reconstructing villages call for on ever increasing number of educated workers and so on. Such educated leaders should not only possess the right type of attitude and outlook to work with the villages. They should imbibe missionary zeal for rural service, develop and taste for the simple rural life and should understand the conditions and problems of rural areas and be responsive to the needs of rural people. They should possess ability to motivate people, mobilise them for co-operative efforts and inculcate in them a spirit of self help and self reliance. They should identify themselves with the interest of rural people and work for their upliftment and resist the temptation to grow parasitic living habit among themselves and perpetuating to grow parasitic living habit among themselves and perpetuating their own previledged position. They should devote their time with heart and soul to raise the rural masses.

The traditional system of education has failed to create such leaders suited to the task of rural reconstruction. They are pre-deminantly Western in their outlook, ultra academic in their programmes and urban in their location and attitudes. Their products are detached from any real relationship to rural needs and conditions. Even rural boys and girls who join the universities and quickly educated and go away from their village origin, depleting rural areas of talented youths. Therefore. a new type of educational institution for rural higher education which could give the rural youth that training, skill and outlook which would make them effective leaders of the rural community only is necessary.

In the beginning of the nineteenth century, though a modernisation was set up to introduce in the education system of India, yet in rural areas, it could surpass the limit of primary schooling. Though in the recent years we notice a growing tencency to establish institutions for secondary education among the rural communities.[2]

But in this case also, to keep the conformity with the changes of our circumstances and to launch a democratic planning, an urgent need to re-orienting and reconstruction is felt in entire rural educational structure which is still lacking. The existing facilities even in primary section are not sufficient and both the primary and secondary education are maintaining a considerable standard still.

Mahatma Gandhi stated in 1936 that

> "If the villages perish, India will perish too. It will be no more India. Her own mission in the world

will get lost. Instead of villages subserving cities, cities must subserve villages''.[3]

The term 'rural' does not imply a mere non-character in spiritial sense. It is social and cultural concept. Rural society has its own social and cultural ethos and, therefore, requires full comprehension of its ingredients while extending the process of development to this vast sector of our people. The rural development is not a negative as a remainder concept of reconstruction the rural society to fully develop its potentialities and capabilities to be self-reliant in basic needs. The word 'rural' thus stands for a socio-cultural entity and is not merely a territorial or locational concept.[4]

ROLE OF NATIONAL COUNCIL FOR RURAL HIGHER EDUCATION

The National Council for Rural Higher Education was established in 1956 in pursuance of the recommedations of the committee on Rural Higher Education with the Headquarters at New Delhi. The Council serves as an expert body to advise the state and central Government about improvement and expansion of rural education in all its phases. It advises the rural educational institutions to act as the co-ordinating agency amongst them. The council examines and appraises proposals in this behalf reffered to, by the Government of India and State Governments and to assist in the implementation of approved programme. It initiates schemes for the development and maintenance of students, higher education in rural areas and to encourage research in problems relating to rural education in all its aspects. The National Council frame its own rules and regulations to regulate matters not covered by the resolution and advice of the Government of India on grants to be paid to institutions participating in the rural development schemes.[5]

RURAL EDUCATION AND UNIVERSITY EDUCATION COMMISSION

To meet the needs of higher education in the villages the Commission of 1948 has recommended a system of rural colleges and Universities. It is suggested that a rural University should include a ring of small residential undergraduate colleges, with specialised and University facilities in the centre. The Commission recommends that the number of students in a residential college should be three hundred and the maximum over all enrolment for colleges and University combined about 25,000.[6]

In rural colleges as in rural secondary schools, general studies should be united with practical courses. Also as with rural secondary students, rural college students should spend about half of their time at studies and half at practical work. Each college as a rule may develop its own industries and other economic activities. The Commission further suggested that industrial training should be given to the rural boys through the rural secondary schools. In fact industrialization of the villages should be one of the fundamental aims of the Rural Higher Education.. If villages are not industrialised, all profitable small scale industries would get concentrated in the towns and cities, and villages would be left with unprofitable operation, and this inevitably would lead to permanent widrawal of the able youngmen from the villages.[7]

Now the Rural Education is on its march. and as a result of the recommendations of University Education Commission the number of colleges have been increased and local people of rural areas have established colleges in different nook and corner. These colleges get encouragement for their development. Though established colleges, most of them have no own building and qualified teachers. As a result students suffer a lot of grivances. In some cases people of the same areas divided into different groups and established colleges by each group and suffered from their real development.

PROBLEMS OF RURAL EDUCATION

We shall now proceed to discuss the problems of rural education as a whole. We have already discussed the problems of some levels of education in the relevant chapters. Here, we analyse the problems of education specially in the rural areas. Many impediments of education in rural areas of the present study have been mentioned here.

Wastage and Stagnation

Wastage and stagnation is the main problem of education in all levels in rural areas. Specially it occurs after one or two years of all the stages, wastage refers to cropping out from the educational institutions and stangnation refers to failure in a class. Stagnation means retention of a student in lower level of all the levels of education. It is possible to stop wastage with the help of special interest of the authority and parents teacher relationship. In order to remove the stagnation the standard of teaching should be improved and made more attractive for children.

Socio-logical Causes

The conservative attitude of our people specially those living in villages is responsible for the slow progress of education. Of the socio-logical factors, the following are but a few educational and cultural backwardness of home, migration of population, low standard of living of parents, growth of families unemployment or underemployment of parents, social and religious prejudices, early marriage, antipathy towards girls education, wide frustration, obsession for education, unrelation to life, ignorance about the ultimate benefits of education and parental indifferences.

Expansion of Education

Our main concern after achieving Independence had been to increase educational facilities, at the primary, secondary and university level. The extension had been quantitative only. The number of schools and colleges has been increased tremendously. New institutions have been started. But no heed has been paid as yet to improve the quality of education at any level.

Rapid Growth of Population

After Independence there has been a remarkable rate of

growth of population. Students' population has increased tremendously. There is always a great rush of admission in the schools and colleges in the beginning of the session. Class sizes of a school and college where extension of buildings is not possible for an average teacher to attend a huge class. Large class sizes have a bad impact on the quality of education.

Lack of Definite Aims of Education

Most of the students know not why they are sent to schools or colleges. The teacher is not aware of the aims of education. There are no clear-cut goals either before the teacher or the taught. Even after fifty years of educational thinking, our educationists and leaders have not been able to decide as to what our goals are.

Inadequate Educational Facilities

In our schools and colleges shortage of material canditions of teaching and equipments create a new problem for teachers and students. The quality of our text books is not satisfactory. Teaching aids are totally lacking. Teachers' guides and teaching materials are not satisfactory. Good qualities of text books are not produced in regional languages for our education system. After the changing of syllabus low standard books occupies the entire area at once. Some of the schools and colleges continue their science section without proper laboratory and equipments.

Defective Methods of Teaching

The methods of teaching in schools, colleges and universities are helpful for the average level students. Educational research in teaching method has nowhere been conducted. The administrative machinery is so rigid that it does not encourage initiative creativity and experimentation. The teaching in may weaker schools and colleges is mechanical and dry. There is no zeal for learning or spirit for discovery in institutions of lower and higher education.

Weak Students Society

Students at every level have one objective before them,

i.e., passing the examination. There is little spirit for learning. There is no enthusism for study and research. Learning for most of them is a mechanical process and involves nothing but memorisation. Self study and discussion are wanting.

Defective Curriculum for Rural Education

As regard curriculum also no serious attempt has been made since the past to revise and reform it in the light of new changes. The problem of curriculum has not been talked radically and no corresponding steps have been taken to improve it for a century. The curriculum does not appear to be related in any way to the real and practical life of the child or its environment.

Indiscipline among Students

The problem of discipline should not be regarded as that of secondary education exclusively, on the other hand. it is a countrywide problem of entire students community. Though the problem of discipline is not directly related to educational organization, yet in our system of education, educational organization, method of teaching and the mode of all combined examinations exercise a profound influence upon the question of discipline as a whole among the students.

Problem of Teachers

Another acute problem of rural education is the problem of teachers in all levels of education. The teacher who do not want to stay in the rural set up due to residential problem. The average efficiency of the teachers has deteriorated, their economic difficulties and lack of social prestige have tended to create in them a sense of frustration. It is no exaggeration to say that incompetent and dissatisfied teachers undermine the very foundation of society. Their incompetence and dissatisfaction affect the students and sow the seeds of revolution, disruption and decay.

No Proper Guidance

There are no facilities for proper educational guidance. In

the absence of educational, vocational and personal guidance wrong choices are often made. The inevitable results is poor achievement and fall in standard.

Standard of Education

It is usually heard today that the general standard of education has shown a downward trend affecting the all levels of education also. Undoubtedly, the policy of the Government has been to expand the quality of education thus ignoring quality, other factors responsible for the low standard of education are the low salary of teachers, most of the teachers being untrained growing discontentment among the teachers towards their profession, abnormal increased of students in the class, the serious lack of necessary requirements and equipments, inefficiency of the managing bodies as well as negligence of educational department to some extent, the wretched financial condition of the institution, abundance of inproper means of reaction as crime of sexfilms, etc., for the students, a growing lack of sense of responsibility among the teachers and their attitude of negligence towards their duties, unsuitability to the text books and indifference and unfamiliarity of the guardian of the students and the general public with the multifarious educational problems. The expansion of education is, no doubt, essential to improve the present backward education condition of the country. But we shall have to take the standard of education into account along with its expansion and ultimately gives preference to Quality' and not 'Quantity' as has been the case so far during the post-Independence period.

Problem of Administration and Co-ordination

Another problem of rural education is the problem of administration and co-ordination. Institutions (School, colleges) are administered by local Body, Government and University in different aspects. Payments and Grants-in-aids are administered by government. Academic side administered and controlled by Board, Council and University and other powers are vested on Managing Committee of Governing Body. Prevailing deplorable condition of internal administration is a major problem of rural education.

CONCLUSION

Above discussions are related with rural education, we have discussed the problems of all levels of education in relavant chapters separately. The aim of rural education is to make the village prosporous, interesting and culturally rich place with such range of opportunity and adventure that young people will find in them, more zest and interest, more cultural advantage, and more opportunity for pioneering there, than in the cities. Cities have drawn the cream of life and culture from the villages, returning almost nothing and thereby reducing the strength of the nation. Education has been progressed in the rural areas. Though the provision made so far cannot be ragarded as adequate, yet it can mention here the opinion of the Rural Higher Education Committee : "There should be no barriers between these institutes and the Universities as there should be none between the villages and towns. It is only when there is a proper give and take between the cities and the villages that both will be enriched."[8]

NOTES

1. Government of India, *Census Report*, 1991. Vol. I.
2. Rawat. p. L., *History of Indian Education*, Ram Prasad and Sons, Agra, 1985. p. 350
3. A.I.U. University News, *Association of India Universities J.I.* 1985, p. 3.
4. *Ibid.*, p. 3.
5. Rawat P.L., *History of Indian Education*, Ram Prased and Sons, Agra, 1985. pp. 350-51
6. Dutta, D., *History of Indian Education*, B. Prakashani, Calcutta. 1969, p. 138.
7. *Ibid.* pp. 138-39.
8. Rawat. P.L., *History of Indian Education*, Ram Prasad and sons, Agra- 3, 1985, p. 351.

Appendices

APPENDIX-A

NATIONAL SCIENCE POLICY

Science policy and decision concerning science now play such a vital role in the national economy and defence that it is most important for the governmental authorities at the highest level to ensure that on major scientific issues they can get advice which is as impartial and objective as it possibly can be. It is important to have an advisory body which is appropriate for this purpose. Such a body should have on it, besides heads of major agencies concerned with scientific research, persons who have a high standing and regard in their professions and who inspire general confidence — a proportion of these members should be distinguished young scientists in their thirties. The number of such persons should not be less than the agency heads. They could be from the universities, research institutions (government or non-government), industry and public life. The advisory body should also have on it not only scientists and technologists but also economists and social scientists and persons with experience of industry and management.

A fundamental concern of science research policy is the relative allocation of priorities with reference to different sectors of scientific effort, both in terms of subjects and in terms of operating agencies. This is a problem which involves vital scientific issues, but it goes beyond science. It involves important economic and political considerations. The resources in men and material available at any time for R&D are severely limited. This is so even for affluent countries. The number of able scientists and engineers is often the critical factor in determining the total volume of the R and D effort. Difficult and sometimes unpleasant choices have to be made among the many competing claims on the use of the available talent and professional manpower. This is inevitable, and a responsibility which cannot be shirked. To lay down effective and operational priorities is not at all an easy thing. It needs a relatively well-defined formation of the national goals and objectives, and it needs hard, courageous and imaginative thinking.

The present Scientific Advisory Committee to the Cabinet cannot perhaps be considered to have effectively performed the functions envisaged above, no matter what its terms of reference are. The Committee is mainly constituted of representatives of the important research organizations in the country. This makes, to say the least, an objective and critical examination of issues of national research policy difficult. The members are often too directly involved to be able to take an objective and detached view. In most of the advanced countries the top Advisory Committee is composed of people who have no 'vested interests' in an institution to defend or to fight for.

We recommend that the Scientific Advisory Committee be reorganized and provided with an effective secretariat with a professional component adequate to its tasks. The Committee should be in a position to assess the broad scientific needs of the country including the universities and advise government on science policy and allocation of total resources between different sectors of scientific activities. The task of this body should be to review continuously the national research policy situation.

Recently the Atomic Energy Department has undertaken a programme for research in radio astronomy and also in the field of molecular biology. The interest of the AEC in these fields is to be welcomed. But it needs to be stressed that these fields of research should primarily be developed and supported in the universities unless there be compelling reasons to the contrary (we are not aware of such reasons).

We should like at this stage to say a word about the Research Councils. We have the Council of Scientific and Industrial Research, the Indian Council of Agricultural Research, the Medical Research Council and the Defence Research Council. It is our view that bodies concerned with science policy and implementation and which have executive and managerial functions requiring detailed and expert examination of diverse issues should ordinarily have professional scientists, engineers or science administrators of high standing as their chairmen.

We may mention that in most of the scientifically advanced countries the organization at the national and governmental levels of research has undergone drastic changes during the last five years or so. In the UK, following the Trend Committee Report, the Department of Scientific and Industrial Research (which corresponds to the CSIR) has been completely overhauled. In its place there has been constituted the Science Research Council which deals with those functions of the DSIR which were concerned with basic research, fellowship awards and research grants to universities. Several of the DSIR laboratories, including the National Physical Laboratory have been transferred to the new Ministry of Technology with a view to bringing the laboratories into closer relationship with industry. The AEC is with the Ministry of Technology. There is also an Advisory Council on Science Policy.

It should be a major task of the national research policy, and policies of the universities to provide a 'climate' conducive to research, and to prevent and eliminate, through energetic and public measures, all dangers and infringements of autonomy and freedom of action in research. It should be recognized that all this needs deliberate effort, and it also takes time. To quote Michael Polyani : 'Those who have visited the parts of the world where scientific life is just beginning, know the back-breaking struggle that the lack of scientific tradition imposes on the pioneers. Here research work stagnates for lack of stimulus, there it runs wild in the absence of any proper directive influence. Unsound reputation grows like mushrooms, based on nothing but commonplace achievements, or even more on empty boasts....However, rich the fund of local genius may be, such environments will fail to bring it to fruition.

In the case of scientific work, zest and enthusiasm of high quality are extremely important. This needs freedom from petty worries and distractions, a proper research climate and a good morale among scientists. It is no easy thing to build scientific institutions with international reputation. These demand single-minded effort, devotion and dedication.

In determining our priorities for research we should be guided by our own national needs and not be unduly influenced by what may happen to be the current fashion in science. If space research and nuclear physics are given a high place in a nation's programme of research, it will be futile to expect that the young talent will elect agriculture or industrial research. If marble floors and possession of expensive equipment become the outer symbols of scientific status, a waste of national resources in the name of science and research becomes almost inevitable. Fred Hoyle has observed : 'People who work in marvellous buildings are dominated by those buildings, whereas it is the other way round for people who work in rabbit warrens. The builders of the great European cathedrals knew this perfectly well. Walk into a big cathedral and it wipes your brain clean of all thoughts. The same thing happens when you walk into these wonderful modern office blocks. The same thing happens all too easily in big science'.

Source : Kothari Commission 1964-66-NCERT, 1971, pp. 764-66.

APPENDIX-B
NATIONAL ACADEMY OF SCIENCE

In the scientific life of a country a national organization or academy of sciences occupies an exceedingly important place. In some ways its role is crucial for the growth of science education and research. While this is not the place to go into the subject at any length, we feel that a brief reference is necessary.

In India the role of a National Academy is performed partly by the National Institute of Sciences. However, it may need some drastic reorganization, if the Institute is to exercise a vigorous leadership in science and play a more significant role in the scientific activities of the nation. In recent decades the demarcation between science and technology has become increasingly thin and artificial, and for this and other reasons, it may be desirable to widen the scope of the fellowship and bring into the Institute more engineers and technologists. Further, if the Institute is to be seriously concerned with the interaction between science, economic growth and national development, it would be useful to extend the fellowship to economists and social scientists. This is the practice in several academies, the most important being the Soviet Academy of Science.

In the above context, we may refer also the Science Council of Japan established after World War II, as it has some features which could perhaps be usefully incorporated in our own organizations. The Council is the legal and official representative body of the scientists of Japan : The JSC has no direct control over research. Its function is to determine what is best for science in Japan and to advise government accordingly. It is under the jurisdiction of the Prime Minister. It has seven divisions : (1) literature, philosophy, pedagogy, psychology and sociology, history; (2) law, political science; (3) economics, commerce and business administration; (4) pure science; (5) engineering; (6) agriculture; (7) medicine, dentistry, pharmacology. The 210 members of the Council, 30 from each of the seven divisions, hold office for three years. They are elected by a nationwide constituency of electors who are either graduates of at least two years' standing or possess five or more years of actual research experience. The Council has a Management Committee of 31 members. The constitution of the Japanese Council is highly democratic. In these days when science impinges on broad issues of economic and national policies, it is desirable that a national organization of scientists is not controlled entirely by the scientific aristocracy, as it were, but the entire scientific community gets a chance to participate in the life and work of the organization.

Many of the major issues of science policy involve considerations which go outside the strict domain of science. In view of this, and other reasons, it is an advantage for a national organization which claims to speak on behalf of the scientific community to involve in its deliberations some elected representatives of the entire fraternity of science. For a country of the size of India it may not be possible to adopt the pattern of the Science Council of Japan, but the possibility could be explored of associating with the National Institute of Sciences a small number of scientists (not fellows of the Institute) elected by the scientific community. The number of such members could be limited to about one third of the total strength of the Council. Such an arrangement would help the process of activization of science by bringing closer contact and participation between its different components.

A national academy has also a major function in promoting international relations in science. Such a body represents the country on international scientific organizations such as the International Council of Scientific Unions and its various committees. India is almost the solitary case of a country which is not represented on the ICSU by a professional academy but by the Government. It is worth mentioning that science academies often help in furthering cooperation between countries amongst which political relations may not be normal.

Source : Kothari Commission 1964-66. NCERT, 1971, pp. 766-68.

APPENDIX-C
UNIVERSITIES IN INDIA

S.No.	Name of the Universities	Year of Establishment	Location/ State
1	2	3	4
1.	Calcutta University, Calcutta	1857	West Bengal
2.	Bombay University, Bombay	1857	Maharashtra
3.	Madras University, Madras	1857	Tamilnadu
4.	Allahabad University, Allahabad	1887	U.P.
5.	Banaras Hindu University, Varanasi	1916	U.P.
6.	Mysore University, Mysore	1916	Mysore
7.	Patna University, Patna	1917	Bihar
8.	Osmania University, Hyderabad	1918	Andhra Pradesh
9.	Aligarh Muslim University, Aligarh	1920	U.P.
10.	University of Lucknow, Lucknow	1921	U.P.
11.	Delhi University, Delhi	1922	Delhi
12.	Nagpur University, Nagpur	1923	Maharashtra
13.	Andhra University, Waltair	1926	A.P.
14.	Agra University, Agra	1927	U.P.
15.	Annamalai University, Annamalai Nagar	1929	A.P.
16.	Kerala University, Tribundrum	1937	Kerala
17.	Utkal University, Bhubaneshwar	1943	Orissa
18.	University of Saugarh, Saugar	1946	M.P.
19.	Rajasthan University, Jaipur	1947	Rajasthan
20.	Punjab University, Chandigarh	1947	Punjab
21.	Guwahati University, Guwahati	1948	Assam
22.	Kashmir University, Srinagar	1948	Kashmir
23.	University of Roorkee, Roorkee	1949	U.P.
24.	University of Pune, Pune	1949	Maharashtra
25.	M.S. University, Baroda	1949	Gujarat
26.	Karnataka University, Dharwar	1949	Karnataka
27.	Gujarat University, Ahmedabad	1950	Gujarat
28.	S.N.D.T. Women's University, Bombay	1951	Maharashtra

1	2	3	4
29.	Vishwa Bharati, Santiniketan	1951	West Bengal
30.	University of Bihar, Muzaffarpur	1952	Bihar
31.	Sri Venkateswara University, Tirupati	1954	Tirupati
32.	Sardar Patel University, Vallabh Vidyanagar	1955	V. Vidyanagar
33.	Jadavpur University, Calcutta	1955	W.B.
34.	Kurukshetra University, Kurukshetra	1956	Haryana
35.	Indira Kala Sangit Viswavidyalaya, Khairagarh	1956	M.P.
36.	Vikram University, Ujjain	1957	M.P.
37.	Gorakhpur University, Gorakhpur	1957	U.P.
38.	Jabalpur University, Jabalpur	1957	M.P.
39.	Sampurnanand Sanskrit Viswavidyalaya	1958	U.P.
40.	Marathawada University, Aurangabad	1958	Maharashtra
41.	University of Burdowan, Burdowan	1960	W.B.
42.	G.B. Pant University of Agriculture and Technology Pantnagar	1960	U.P.
43.	Bhagalpur University, Bhagalpur	1960	Bihar
44.	Ranchi University, Ranchi	1960	Bihar
45.	Kalyani University, Kalyani	1960	W.B.
46.	K.S.D. Sanskrit Viswavidyalaya, Darbhanga	1961	Bihar
47.	Magadh University, Bodh Gaya	1962	Bihar
48.	Punjabi University, Patiala	1962	Punjab
49.	Rabindra Bharati University, Calcutta	1962	W.B.
50.	North Bengal University, Raja Rammohanpur	1962	W.B.
51.	University of Jodhpur, Jodhpur	1962	Rajasthan
52.	Orissa University of Agriculture and Technology (Bhubaneswar)	1962	Orissa
53.	University of Udaipur, Udaipur	1962	Rajasthan
54.	Punjab Agricultural University, Ludhiana	1962	Punjab

1	2	3	4
55.	Shivaji University, Kolhapur	1962	Maharashtra
56.	Kashi Vidyapith, Varanashi	1963	U.P.
57.	University of Indore, Indore	1964	M.P.
58.	Jiwaji University, Gwalior	1964	M.P.
59.	Ravishankar University, Raipur	1964	M.P.
60.	University of Agricultural Sciences, Bangalore	1964	Karnataka
61.	A.P. Agricultural University, Hyderabad	1964	A.P.
62.	Bangalore University, Bangalore	1964	Karnataka
63.	J.N. Krishi Viswavidyalaya, Jabalpur	1964	M.P.
64.	Dibrugarh University, Dibrugarh	1965	Assam
65.	Kanpur University, Kanpur	1966	U.P.
66.	Madurai University, Madurai	1966	Tamilnadu
67.	Meerut University, Meerut	1966	U.P.
68.	Gujarat Ayurvedic University, Jamnagar	1966	Gujarat
69.	Behrampur University, Behrampur	1967	Orissa
70.	Saurastra University, Rajkot	1967	Gujarat
71.	Sambalpur University, Sambalpur	1967	Orissa
72.	South Gujarat University, Surat	1967	Gujarat
73.	Mahtma Phule Krishi Viswavidyalaya, Ahmednagar	1967	Maharashtra
74.	Awadesh Pratap Singh University, Rewa	1968	Madhya Pradesh
75.	University of Calicut, Calicut	1968	Kerala
76.	Assam Agricultural University, Jorhat	1968	Assam
77.	Jawaharlal Nehra University, Delhi	1968/69	Delhi
78.	Jammu University, Jammu	1969	J.&K.
79.	Panjabrao Krishi Vidyapith, Akola	1969	Maharashtra
80.	Guru Nanak University, Amritsar	1969	Punjab
81.	Haryana Agricultural University	1970	Hissar (Haryana)
82.	Himachal Pradesh University, Shimla	1970	Himachal Pradesh
83.	Bhopal Viswavidyalaya, Bhopal	1970	Madhya Pradesh

1	2	3	4
84.	Tamilnadu Agricultural University, Coimbatore	1971	Tamilnadu
85.	Rajendra Agricultural University, Samastipur	1971	Bihar (Pusa)
86.	University of Cochin, Cochin	1971	Kerala
87.	Kerala Agricultural University, Mannuthy	1971	Kerala (Trissur)
88.	L.N. Mithila University, Darbhanga	1972	Bihar
89.	Marathwada Krishi Viyapith, Parbhani	1972	Maharashtra
90.	Kankan Krishi Vidyapith, Dapali, Ratnagiri	1972	Maharashtra
91.	Gujarat Agricultural University, Ahmedabad	1972	Gujarat
92.	J.N. Technological University, Hyderabad	1972	Andhra Pradesh
93.	North Eastern Hills University, Shillong	1973	Meghalaya
94.	University of Garwal, Srinagar	1973	Uttar Pradesh
95.	University of Kumaon, Nainital	1973	Uttar Pradesh
96.	Bidhan Chandra Krishi Viswa Vidyalaya, Kalyani	1974	West Bengal
97.	University of Hyderabad, Hyderabad	1974	Andhra Pradesh
98.	Nalsor University of Law, Hyderabad	NA	Andhra Pradesh
99.	Mohanlal Sukadia University, Udaipur	NA	Rajasthan
100.	Rajiv Gandhi Technological University, Bhopal	1998	Madhya Pradesh
101.	Tezpur University, Tezpur	1994-5	Assam
102.	Assam University, Silchar	1994-5	Assam
103.	Manipur University, Manipur	1980	Manipur
104.	Arunachal Pradesh University, Itanagar	NA	Arunachal Pradesh
105.	Tripura University,	NA	Tripura
106.	Potti Sriramula Telegu University, Hyderabad	NA	Andhra Pradesh
107.	Rajiv Gandhi University of Health Sciences, Karnataka	NA	Karnataka
108.	Periyar University, Salem	NA	Tamilnadu

1	2	3	4
109.	Tamilnadu Veterinary and Animal Sciences University, Chennai	NA	Tamilnadu
110.	Hamdard University, Hamdard Nagar	NA	New Delhi
111.	Bundelkhand University	1975	Uttar Pradesh
112.	Anna University, Chennai	1978	Tamilnadu
113.	Vidyasagar University, Midnapur	NA	West Bengal
114.	Dr. B.R. Ambedkar University	NA	—
115.	Maharishi Mahesh Yogi Vedic Viswavidyalaya	1995	Madhya Pradesh
116.	Kakatiya University	1976	Andhra Pradesh
117.	Nagarjuna University	1976	Andhra Pradesh
118.	Srikrishna Devaraya University	1981	Andhra Pradesh
119.	Birsa Agricultural University	1981	Bihar
120.	Bhavanagar University, Bhabanagar	1979	Gujarat
121.	Maharishi Dayananda University	1976	Haryana
122.	H.P. Agricultural University	1978	Himachal Pradesh
123.	Gulbarga University	1980	Karnataka
124.	Mangalore University	1980	Karnataka
125.	Sri. Jagannath Sanskrit Viswavidyalaya	1981	Coimbatore
126.	Bharathian University, Coimbatore (Tamilnadu)	1982	Tamilnadu
127.	Bharatidasan University, Tiruchirapalli	1982	Tamilnadu
128.	Tamil University	1981	Tamilnadu
129.	Abadh University	1975	Uttar Pradesh
130.	Chandrashekhar Azad University of Agriculture and Technology	1974	Uttar Pradesh
131.	Narendradeo University of Agriculture and Technology	1974	Uttar Pradesh
132.	Rohilkhand University	1975	Uttar Pradesh
133.	Allagappa University, Alagappa Nagar, Karaikudi	NA	Karaikudi
134.	Amarabati University, Amarabati	NA	Amarabati
135.	Chitrakut Gramoday Viswavidyalaya, Chitrakut	NA	Chitrakut

1	2	3	4
136.	Cochin University of Science and Technology	NA	Kerala
137.	Dr. Babasaheb Ambedkar Technological University	NA	Lonere
138.	Dr. Y.S. Parmar University of Horticulture and Forestry	NA	Nauni
139.	Goa University, Tabigao Plateau	NA	Goa
140.	Guru Ghasidas University, Bilaspur	NA	Bilaspur
141.	Jaiprakash University, Chapra	NA	Bihar
142.	Jain Viswabharati Institute, Ladnun	NA	Ladnun
143.	Kuvempu University, Shimoga	NA	Karnataka
144.	Maharshi Dayananda Saraswati University, Ajmer	NA	Rajasthan
145.	Mahatma Gandhi University,	NA	Kottayam
146.	Manonmaniam Sundaranar University, Tirunelveli	NA	Tamilnadu
147.	Mother Teresa Women's University, Madras	NA	Tamilnadu
148.	National Law School of India University, Bangalore	NA	Karnataka
149.	Pandit Ravishankar Shukla University, Raipur	NA	Raipur
150.	Rastriya Sanskrit Vidyapith, Tirupati	NA	Tirupati
151.	Sher-e-Kashmir University of Agriculture Science and Technology	NA	Kashmir
152.	L.B. Shastri Rastriya Sanskrit Vidyapith, New Delhi	NA	Delhi
153.	Krishnadevaraya University, Anantapur	NA	Anantapur
154.	Padmabati Mahila Viswavidyalayam, Tirupati	NA	Tirupati
155.	Telegu University, Hyderabad	NA	Andhra Pradesh
156.	Guru Jambeshwar University, Hissar	NA	Haryana

Sources : (i) *University Grants Commission Report*, (ii) *University News*, AIU, Feb. 7-2000, (iii) *Status Report Series*, AIU, 1986.

APPENDIX-D
OPEN UNIVERSITIES IN INDIA

S.No.	Name of the Institutions	Year of Establishment	Location
1	2	3	4
1.	Dr. B.R. Ambedkar Open University, Jubilee Hills, Hyderabad-500 033	1982	Andhra Pradesh
2.	Indira Gandhi National Open University, Maidan Garhi, New Delhi-110 068	1985	New Delhi
3.	State Open University, Manash-Gongotri, Mysore-570 006	1996	Mysore
4.	Nalanda Open University, Adarsh Colony, Patna-800 001	1987	Bihar
5.	Jasowanta Rao Chavan Maharashtra Open University, Dayan-Gongotri, Nasik-422 005	1989	Maharashtra
6.	Kota Open University, Akhelgar, Kota-324 010	1987	Kota
7.	Madhyapradesh Open University, Bhopal	NA	Madhya Pradesh
8.	Gujrat Open University, Ahmedabad	NA	Gujarat
9.	Netaji Subhash Open University, Woodburn Park, Calcutta-700 020	1999	West Bengal

Source : (i) *University Grants Commission Report*, (ii) *University News*, AIU, (iii) *Hand-book of Distance Education*, AIU.

APPENDIX-E

INSTITUTIONS DEEMED TO BE UNIVERSITIES IN INDIA

S.No.	Name of the Institutions	Establishment year	Year, declared as a deemed to be University	State
1.	Gurukul Kangri Viswavidyalaya, Hardwar	1900	1961	U.P.
2.	Indian Agricultural Research Institute, Delhi	1905	1958	Delhi
3.	Indian Institute of Science, Bangalore	1909	1958	Karnataka
4.	Jamia Milia Islamia, New Delhi	1920	1961	Delhi
5.	Gujrat Vidyapith, Ahmedbad	1920	1963	Gujarat
6.	Indian School of Mines, Dhanbad	1926	1967	Bihar
7.	Tata Institute of Social Sciences, Bombay	1936	1964	Maharashtra
8.	Central Institute of English and Foreign Languages, Hyderabad	1958	1973	Andhra Pradesh
9.	Birla Institute of Technology and Sciences, Pilani	1964	1964	Rajasthan
10.	Birla Institute of Technology, Mesra, Ranchi	NA	NA	Bihar
11.	Bharati Vidyapith, Pune	NA	NA	Maharashtra
12.	Gandhigram Rural Institute, Gandhigram	NA	NA	Tamilnadu
13.	Rajasthan Vidyapith			Rajasthan
14.	Forest Research Institute, Dehradun	NA	1991	U.P.

Sources : (i) *University Grants Commission Report*, 1997-98.

(ii) *University News*, February 7, 2000.

(iii) *Higher Education in India*, AIU.

(iv) *University News*, February 7, 2000.

APPENDIX-F

INSTITUTIONS OF NATIONAL IMPORTANCE IN INDIA

S.No.	Name of the Institutions	Establishment year	National Importance year	State
1.	Hindi Sahitya Sammelan, Allahabad (Prayag)	1910	1962	U.P.
2.	Dakshin Bharati Hindi Prachar Sabha, Chennai	1918	1964	T.N.
3.	Indian Statistical Institute, Calcutta	1932	1959	W.B.
4.	Indian Institute of Technology, Kharagpur	1950	1956	W.B.
5.	All India Institute of Medical Sciences, New Delhi	1956	1956	Delhi
6.	Indian Institute of Technology, Bombay	1958	1962	Maharashtra
7.	Indian Institute of Technology, Madras	1959	1962	T.N.
8.	Indian Institute of Technology, Kanpur	1959	1962	U.P.
9.	Indian Institute of Technology, Delhi	1961	1963	Delhi
10.	Post Graduate Institute of Medical Education and Research, Chandigarh	1962	1967	Punjab
11.	Indian Institute of Technology Guwahati (North Guwahati)	1987	—	Assam

Sources : (i) *University Grants Commission Report*, 1997-98.

(ii) *Status Report Series*, A.I.U. (Internal Management in Universities), 1986.

(iii) *University News*, February 7, 2000.

(iv) *University News*, March 13, 2000.

APPENDIX-G

UNIVERSITIES AND INSTITUTIONS OF HIGHER LEARNING IN INDIA (STATE-WISE)

ANDHRA

1. Acharya N.G. Ranga Agricultural University, Hyderabad
2. Andhra University, Visakhapatnam
3. Central Institute of English & Foreign Languages, Hyderabad
4. Dr. B.R. Ambedkar Open University, Hyderabad
5. Dravidian University, Kuppam
6. University of Hyderabad, Hyderabad
7. Jawaharlal Nehru Technological University, Hyderabad
8. Kakatiya University, Warangal
9. Maulana Azad National Urdu University, Hyderabad
10. Nagarjuna University, Guntur
11. Nizam's Institute of Medical Sciences, Hyderabad
12. NTR University of Health Sciences, Vijayawada
13. Osmania University, Hyderabad
14. Potti Sreeramulu Telugu University, Hyderabad
15. Rashtriya Sanskrit Vidyapeetha, Tirupati
16. Sri Krishnadevaraya University, Anantapur
17. Sri Padmavati Mahila Vishvavidyalayam, Tirupati
18. Sri Sathya Sai Institute of Higher Learning, Anantapur
19. Sri Venkateswara Institute of Medical Sciences, Tirupati
20. Sri Venkateswara University, Tirupati

ARUNACHAL PRADESH

21. Arunachal University, Itanagar

ASSAM

22. Assam Agricultural University, Jorhat
23. Assam University, Silchar
24. Dibrugarh University, Dibrugarh
25. Guwahati University, Guwahati
26. Indian Institute of Technology, Guwahati
27. Tezpur University, Tezpur

BIHAR

28. B.N. Mandal University, Madhepura

29. Babasaheb Bhimrao Ambedkar Bihar University, Muzaffarpur
30. Birla Institute of Technology, Ranchi
31. Birsa Agricultural University, Ranchi
32. Indian School of Mines, Dhanbad
33. Jai Prakash Vishwavidyalaya, Chapra
34. Kameshwar Singh Darbhanga Sanskrit University, Darbhanga
35. Lalit Narayan Mithila University, Darbhanga
36. Magadh University, Bodh Gaya
37. Nalanda Open University, Patna
38. Patna University, Patna
39. Rajendra Agricultural University, Pusa, Samastipur
40. Ranchi University, Ranchi
41. Siddhu Kanhu University, Dumka
42. Tilka Manjhi Bhagalpur University, Bhagalpur
43. Veer Kunwar Singh University, Arrah
44. Vinoba Bhave University, Hazaribag

CHANDIGARH

45. Panjab University, Chandigarh
46. Postgraduate Institute of Medical Education & Research, Chandigarh

DELHI

47. All India Institute of Medical Sciences, New Delhi
48. University of Delhi, Delhi
49. Indian Agricultural Research Institute, New Delhi
50. Indian Institute of Technology, New Delhi
51. Indira Gandhi National Open University, New Delhi
52. Jamia Hamdard, New Delhi
53. Jamia Millia Islamia, New Delhi
54. Jawaharlal Nehru University, New Delhi
55. National Museum Institute of History of Art, Conservation & Museology, New Delhi
56. School of Planning & Architecture, New Delhi
57. Shri Lal Bahadur Shastri Rashtriya Sanskrit Vidyapeeth, New Delhi

GOA

58. Goa University, Goa

GUJARAT

59. Bhavnagar University, Bhavnagar
60. Dr. Babasaheb Ambedkar Open University, Ahmedabad
61. Gujarat Agricultural University, Dantiwada
62. Gujarat Ayurved University, Jamnagar
63. Gujarat University, Ahmedabad
64. Gujarat Vidyapith, Ahmedabad
65. M. S. University of Baroda, Vadodara
66. North Gujarat University, Patna
67. Sardar Patel University, Vallabh Vidyanagar
68. Saurashtra University, Rajkot
69. South Gujarat University, Surat

HARYANA

70. Ch. Charan Singh Haryana Agricultural University, Hisar
71. Guru Jambheshwar University, Hisar
72. Kurukshetra University, Kurukshetra
73. Maharshi Dayanand University, Rohtak
74. National Dairy Research Institute, Karnal

HIMACHAL PRADESH

75. Dr. Y.S. Parmar University of Horticulture & Forestry, Solan
76. Himachal Pradesh Krishi Vishwavidyalaya, Palampur
77. Himachal Pradesh University, Shimla

J & K

78. University of Jammu, Jammu
79. University of Kashmir, Srinagar
80. Sher-e-Kashmir University of Agricultural Sciences & Technology, Srinagar

KARNATAKA

81. University of Agricultural Sciences, Bangalore
82. University of Agricultural Sciences, Dharwad
83. University of Bangalore, Bangalore
84. Gulbarga University, Gulbarga
85. Indian Institute of Science, Bangalore
86. Kannada University, Kamalapura

87. Karnataka State Open University, Mysore
88. Karnatak University, Dharwad
89. Kuvempu University, Shimoga
90. Mangalore University, Mangalore
91. Manipal Academy of Higher Education, Manipal
92. University of Mysore, Mysore
93. National Institute of Mental Health & Neuro Sciences, Bangalore
94. National Law School of India University, Bangalore
95. Rajiv Gandhi University of Health Sciences, Bangalore

KERALA

96. University of Calicut, Kozhikode
97. Cochin University of Science & Technology, Kochi
98. Kannur University, Kannur
99. University of Kerala, Thiruvananthapuram
100. Kerala Agricultural University, Thrissur
101. Mahatma Gandhi University, Kottayam
102. Sree Chitra Tirunal Institute for Medical Sciences & Technology, Thiruvananthapuram
103. Sree Shankaracharya University of Sanskrit, Kalady
104. Visveswaraiah Technological University, Belgaum

MADHYA PRADESH

105. Awadhesh Pratap Singh University, Rewa
106. Barkatullah Vishwavidyalaya, Bhopal
107. Devi Ahilya Vishwavidyalaya, Indore
108. Dr. Harisingh Gour Vishwavidyalaya, Sagar
109. Guru Ghasidas University, Bilaspur
110. Indira Gandhi Krishi Vishwavidyalaya, Raipur
111. Indira Kala Sangit Vishwavidyalaya, Khairagarh
112. Jawaharlal Nehru Krishi Vishwavidyalaya, Jabalpur
113. Jiwaji University, Gwalior
114. Lakshmi Bai National Institute of Physical Education, Gwalior
115. Madhya Pradesh Bhoj University, Bhopal
116. Maharishi Mahesh Yogi Vedic Vishwavidyalaya, Jabalpur
117. Mahatma Gandhi Gramodya Vishwavidyalaya, Chitrakoot
118. Makhanlal Chaturvedi National University of Journalism, Bhopal
119. Pandit Ravishankar Shukla University, Raipur

120. Rani Durgavati Vishwavidyalaya, Jabalpur
121. Vikram University, Ujjain

MAHARASHTRA

122. Amravati University, Amravati
123. Bharati Vidyapeeth, Pune
124. Central Institute of Fisheries Education, Mumbai
125. Decan College Post Graduate & Research Institute, Pune
126. Dr. Babasaheb Ambedkar Marathwada University, Aurangabad
127. Dr. Babasaheb Ambedkar Tchnological University, Lonere
128. Dr. Panjabrao Deshmukh Krishi Vidyapeeth, Akola
129. Gokhale Institute of Politics & Economics, Pune
130. Indian Institute of Technology, Mumbai
131. Indira Gandhi Institute of Development Research, Mumbai
132. International Institute of Population Sciences, Mumbai
133. Kavikulguru Kalidas Sanskrit Vishwavidyalaya, Ramtek
134. Konkan Krishi Vidyapeeth, Dapoli
135. Mahatma Gandhi Antarrashtriya Hindi Vishwavidyalaya, Wardha
136. Mahatma Phule Krishi Vidyapeeth, Rahuri
137. Marathwada Krishi Vidyapeeth, Parbhani
138. University of Mumbai, Mumbai
139. Nagpur University, Nagpur
140. North Maharashtra University, Jalgaon
141. University of Pune, Pune
142. Shivaji University, Kolhapur
143. SNDT Women's University, Mumbai
144. Swami Ramanand Teerth Marathwada University, Nanded
145. Tata Institute of Social Sciences, Mumbai
146. Tilak Maharashtra Vidyapeeth, Pune
147. Yashwantrao Chavan Maharashtra Open University, Nashik

MANIPUR

148. Central Agricultural University, Imphal
149. Manipur University, Imphal

MEGHALAYA

150. North Eastern Hill University, Shillong

NAGALAND

151. Nagaland University, Kohima

ORISSA

152. Berhampur University, Berhampur
153. Orissa University of Agriculture & Technology, Bhubaneswar
154. Sambalpur University, Sambalpur
155. Shri Jagannath Sanskrit Viswavidyalaya, Puri
156. Utkal University, Bhubaneswar

PONDICHERRY

157. Pondicherry University, Pondicherry

PUNJAB

158. Guru Nanak Dev University, Amritsar
159. Punjab Agricultural University, Ludhiana
160. Punjab Technical University, Jalandhar
161. Punjabi University, Patiala
162. Thapar Institute of Engineering & Technology, Patiala

RAJASTHAN

163. Banasthali Vidyapith, Banasthali
164. Birla Institute of Technology & Science, Pilani
165. Jai Narain Vyas University, Jodhpur
166. Jain Vishva Bharati Institute, Ladnun
167. Kota Open University, Kota
168. Maharshi Dayanand Saraswati University, Ajmer
169. Mohanlal Sukhadia University, Udaipur
170. Rajasthan Agricultural University, Bikaner
171. University of Rajasthan, Jaipur
172. Rajasthan Vidyapeeth, Udaipur

SIKKIM

173. Sikkim-Manipal University of Health, Medical & Technological Sciences, Gangtok

TAMIL NADU

174. Alagappa University, Karaikudi
175. Anna University, Chennai
176. Annamalai University, Annamalainagar

177. Avinashilingam Institute for Home Science & Higher Education for Women, Coimbatore
178. Bharathiar University, Coimbatore
179. Bharathidasan University, Tiruchirapalli
180. Dakshina Bharat Hindi Prachar Sabha, Chennai
181. Gandhigram Rural Institute, Gandhigram
182. Indian Institute of Technology, Chennai
183. University of Madras, Chennai
184. Madurai Kamaraj University, Madurai
185. Manonmaniam Sundaranar University, Tirunelveli
186. Mother Teresa Women's University, Kodaikanal
187. Periyar University, Salem
188. Sri Chandrasekhareadra Saraswathi Viswa Maha Vidyalaya, Kancheepuram
189. Sri Ramachandra Medical College & Research Institute, Chennai
190. Tamil Nadu Agricultural University, Coimbatore
191. Tamil Nadu Dr. Ambedkar Law University, Chennai
192. Tamil Nadu Dr. M.G.R. Medical University, Chennai
193. Tamil Nadu Veterinary & Animal Sciences University, Chennai
194. Tamil University, Thanjavur

TRIPURA

195. Tripura University, Agartala

UTTAR PRADESH

196. Aligarh Muslim University, Aligarh
197. University of Allahabad, Allahabad
198. Babasaheb Bhimrao Ambedkar University, Lucknow
199. Banaras Hindu University, Varanasi
200. University of Bundelkhand, Jhansi
201. Central Institute of Higher Tibetan Studies, Varanasi
202. Ch. Charan Singh University, Meerut
203. Chandra Shekhar Azad University of Agriculture & Technology, Kanpur
204. Chhatrapati Shahu Ji Maharaj Kanpur University, Kanpur
205. Dayallbagh Educational Institute, Agra
206. Deen Dayal Upadhyaya Gorakhpur University, Gorakhpur
207. Dr. Bhim Rao Ambedkar University, Agra

208. Dr. Ram Manohar Lohia Awadh University, Faizabad
209. Forest Research Institute, Dehradun
210. Govind Ballabh Pant University of Agriculture & Technology, Pantnagar
211. Gurukula Kangri Vishwavidyalaya, Hardwar
212. Hemwati Nandan Bahuguna Garhwal University, Srinagar
213. Indian Institute of Technology, Kanpur
214. Indian Veterinary Research Institute, Izatnagar
215. Kumaun University, Nainital
216. University of Lucknow, Lucknow
217. Mahatma Gandhi Kashi Vidyapeeth, Varanasi
218. M.J.P. Rohilkhand University, Bareilly
219. Narendra Deva University of Agriculture and Technology, Faizabad
220. Purvanchal University, Jaunpur
221. University of Roorkee, Roorkee
222. Sampurnanand Sanskrit Vishwavidyalaya, Varanasi
223. Sanjay Gandhi Postgraduate Postgraduate Institute of Medical Sciences, Lucknow

WEST BENGAL

224. Bengal Engineering College, Howrah
225. Bidhan Chandra Krishi Vishwavidyalaya, Mohanpur
226. University of Burdwan, Burdwan
227. University of Calcutta, Calcutta
228. Indian Institute of Technology, Kharagpur
229. Indian Statistical Institute, Calcutta
230. Jadavpur University, Calcutta
231. University of Kalyani, Kalyani
232. Netaji Subhash Open University, Calcutta
233. Univesity of North Bengal, Darjeeling
234. Rabindra Bharati University, Calcutta
235. Vidyasagar University, Midnapore
236. Visva Bharati, Santiniketan
237. West Bengal University of Animal and Fisheries Sciences, Calcutta

Source. University Institutions in India, Association of Indian Universities, AIU House, 16 Kotla Marg, New Delhi-110 012

Bibliography

A.I.U., *Accountability in Higher Education.*

A.I.U., Delhi, University News December 1, 1982.

A.I.U., *Environmental Challenges in the Universities.*

A.I.U., *Excellence Achieving and Relevance in Higher Education.*

A.I.U., *Higher Education and Development* (Papers), 1975.

A.I.U., *Higher Education in India In Search of Quality.*

A.I.U., *Higher Education in India*, Retrospect and Prospect.

A.I.U., *Policies of Higher Education.*

A.I.U., *University Autonomy its meaning today*, paper 7.

A.I.U., *University News*, August 1, 1980.

A.I.U., *University News*, August 16, 1984.

A.I.U., *University News*, August 8, 1985.

A.I.U., *University News*, December 23, 1984.

A.I.U., *University News*, January 1, 1985.

A.I.U., *University News*, July 16, 1984.

A.I.U., *University News*, May 8, April 8, 1985.

A.I.U., *University News*, September 16, 1984.

A.I.U., *University News*, September 1998.

Agarwal, D.B. & Singh, G., *All India Educational Directory*, 1972.

Ahmed, R., *Forward to the Research Monograph*, 1976.

Arrora, D.S., *History of Education in India*, 1976.

Arthur, M.H., *The Education in India.*

Azad, J.L., *Financing of Higher Education in India.*

Barpujaree, H.K., *A Short History of Higher Education in Assam.*

Best, J.M., *Research in Education*, 1982.

Bhatnagar, Verma, *Educational Administration.*

Bhatta, Mukerjee, and Arora, *History of Education in India.*

Bhattachayya, S., *Methodology of Educational Research.*

Bidner, F.M., *Education in the History of Western Civilization*, 1970.

Biswas and Agarwal, *India Education Document since Independence*, 1971.

Blishen, E., *Education To-day*, 1963.

Brawer, F.B., *New Perspectives of Personality Development in College Students.*

Buch, M.P., *Second Survey of Research in Education.*

Chandrakant, L.S., *Technical Education in India Today*, 1963.

Chatterjee, K.K., *English Education in India.*

Chaube, S.P., *A Text Book of Comperative Education.*

Chaube, S.P., *Features of Comperative Education 1985*, Vinod Pustak Bhander A.2.

Chauhan, D.S., *A Study if University Examination*, 1967.

Connant B. James, *Science and Common Sence*, 1951.

Cotton College, 22-2-82, *Report of the Seminar on Problems of North East*, Technology and New Clear Physics Physics Dept.

Das, K.K., *A Hand Book of Current Problems of Indian Education.*

Das, T.S., *Sanjukta Rajya America Me Siksha.*

Das., L., *A Text Book of Education.*

Dasgupta, N., *Bharatar Siksha Itihas Aru Adhunik Siksha Samasya*, 1970.

Dessai, Dessai, *Some Critical Issues of Higher Education*, 1970.

Deva, Singh Jogindra, *Towards a Sociology of Culture in India.*

Dhar/Singh, *Academic Staff Colleges* (A Developing Concept), Sterling Publishers Pvt. Ltd., 1990.

Dodwell., H.H., Cambridge History of India.

Dubey, R.K., *Towards Democracy and Changes in Education*, 1980.

Dutta, D., *History of Education in India.*

Edgar and Others, "Learning to be", *The World of Education Today and Tomorrow*, 1973.

G. Ram Reddy, *Higher Education in India*, Sterling Publishers Pvt. Ltd., 1995.

G. Ram Reddy, *Open Universities, The Ivory Towers Thrown open.*, Sterling Publishers Pvt. Ltd.

Gandhi K., *Issues and Choices in Higher Education*, 1977.

Gangulee, B.N., *India Year Book*, 1991.

Gangulee, B.N., *Social Development* (Essay of Honour Srimati Durgabai Deshmukh), VoI. 5. No. 1-2, 1975.

Gilchrist, R.N., *Principles of Political Science*, Orient Longman, Madras.

Goswami, D.H., *University Administration in N.E. India*, 1981.

Govt. of India, *Election Directory*, 1983.

Govt. of Assam, *Report, Directorate of Technical Education* (Annual) 1978-79.

Govt. of India, Annual Review of Education in India for 1953-54.

Govt. of India, *Planning Commission Draft*, Plan VI, 1978-83.

Hassan, S.N., *Challenges in Education Culture and Social Welfare*.

Hofstedias, R., *Development and Scope of Higher Education in America*.

Hunt, E.F., *Social Sciences*, p. 631.

Inamdar, N.R., *Educational Administration in Zilla Parishads in Maharastra*, 1974.

Iqbal Narain, 'Visiting lecturer', G.U. Room 1, on *Higher Education Its Dilemma and Problems*.

Joshi, N.C., *Perspectives on Higher Education*.

Journal (Deoghar), *Ramkrishna Mission Vidyapeeth*, 1981.

'Journal' Indian Council of Historical Research Seminar on Archeology, 1985, Guwahati 1.

Kahli, V.K., *Current Problems of India Education*, 1972.

Kapoor, Bose, *Address of Seminars in Current Problems of Indian Education*, Calcutta, 11th March, 1981.

Kapoor, J.N., *Current Issue in Higher Education in India*.

Kapoor, J.N., *Current Issue in World Higher Education*.

Kochar, S.K., *Pivotal Issues in Indian Education*.

Kothari, D.S., *Education Commission Report*, 1964-66.

Kundu/Gupta, *Autonomous Colleges*, Sterling Publishers Pvt. Ltd., 1993.

Lovell and Lowson, *Understanding Research in Education*.

Lulla and Murty, *Essential Problems of Indian Education*.

M. Stuwart, J., *Education documents English and Wales.*

M.G. Reddy, *Higher Education in india*, 1997, A.P.H. Publishing Corporation, New Delhi.

Macmillan, *History of Education in India*, 1951.

Maheswari, S.R., *Local Government in India*, L.N. Agarwal, Agra-3 1984.

Mahmod Syed, *A History of English Education in India.*

Majumdar, S.C., *A Century of Calcutta University Administration*, 1857-1957.

Mank, F.P., *Educational Policy in India.*

Manly, J.G., *The Science of Education Research*, 1964.

Mehra, L.S., *Youth in Modern Society*, 1977.

Misra, D.K., *Youth, University and Community.*

Mohanty, J., *Indian Education in the Emerging Society.*

Mudaliar, L.S., *Report of Education*, 1954.

Mukerjee, S.N, *History of Education in India.*

Mukherjee, S.N., *Education in India Today and Tomorrow.*

Narayan, S., *Education of the Future.*

National Council of Woman Education, VI Annual Report, 1981.

NCERT, 1964, *The Indian Year Book of Education.*

Neog, M., *Biswaridyalaya Vasa, Vassan Aru Vraman.*

New Delhi, *C.A.B.E. Report.*

Newman, H.C., *The Idea of University.*

Nurrullah and Naik, *A Students History of Education in India.*

Oad, Singh and Ruhela, *Perspectives of India Education*, 1975.

P.K. Bose, *Higher Education at Cross Roads*, World Press.

Pauling, L., *Science and World Peace*, 1967.

Prem Kripal, *A Decade of Education in India.*

Prem, Kripal, *Education*, 25.

Premi, M.K., *Educational Planning in India*, 1972.

R.P. Singh, *The Challenge of Tomorrow*, Sterling Publishers Pvt. Ltd., 1993.

Radhakrishnan, S., *University Education Commission*, 1948.

Rai Lazpat, *The Problems of National Education in India.*

Rai, B.C., *Local Self Government in India*, Prakashan Kendra.

Raj, N.R., *Crisis of Higher Education.*

Rawat, P.L., *History of Indian Education.*

Ray, N.R., *Some Current Educational Problems.*

Reddy, V.N.K., *Man Education and Values.*

Reld, J., *New Direction in American University.*

Ruhela, S.P., *Educational Challenges in Socialist India*, 1975.

Russel, B., *The Impact of Science upon Society*, 1953.

S.Kumar and Associates, *Education*, S.Kumar and Associates. July 1984, Lucknow 1.

——, *Education*, Vol. 65, 1 January 1985.

——, *Educational Review*, February 1985.

——, *India Pocket Book of University Education.*

S.N.D.T. (Univ.), *Report of the National Conference on Women Studies, Education*, 1981.

Sadler, M.E., *Report of Education Commission*, 1917.

Safaya, R., *Current Problems of India Education.*

Safaya, R., *Development planning and Problems of Indian Education*, 1982.

Saikia, S., *History of Indian Education*, 1981.

Saikia. S., 'Abstract' *Problems of Education in India.*, 1975.

Saini, S.K., *Development of Education in India.*

Sankar and Ahluwalia, *Research Needs in the Study of Education*, 1968.

Saravai, V., *Science policy and National Development*, 1974.

Sarma, N.R. & Sarma I, *History and Problems of Indian Education.*

Sarma, Prasad, Satya Narayan, *Research Method in Social Sciences*, 1983.

——, *Successful Supervision and Inspection*, 1981.

Sen, N.B., *Progress of Education in India.*

Sen. N.B., *Advancement of Learning in Independent India.*

Sen, N.B., *Glorious thoughts on Education.*

Sengupta, P., *Women Education in India*, 1960.

Shah, A.B., *Higher Education in India.*

Siquria, T.N., *Education in India 1948* (CUP).

Singh, K.N., *A Simple Study of Comperative Local Govt. and Administration*, Ajanta Prakashan, Delhi-6.

Siquira, N.B., *Modern Indian Education.*

'Souvenir', Golden Jubilee Volume, Cotton College, 1950-51.

'Souvenir', *National Academy of Science*, G.U.

Souvenir, Pragjyoutisha (All India Oriental Conference) XXII Session, 1965.

Srinivas, M.N., *Social Change in Modern India.*

Srivastava, L.N., *A Simple Study of Local Self Government in India*, Surjeet Book Depot, Delhi, 1986.

Stephens, M.D. Gardun, *Higher Education Alternatives.*

Subha, B.D., *Towards the New Pattern of Education in India*, 1976.

Sukla, P.D., *Towards the New Pattern of Education in India.*

Sundaram, R.S., *Education a Catastrophe*, 1976.

Suri, M.S., *American Influence on Higher Education in India*, 1979.

Thekaray, V.P., *Education of Women*, 1970.

Thimaiaih, G., *Studies in Rural Development*, 1980.

'Times of India', *Science Today*, January, 1967.

U.G.C., Annual Report for the year, 1988-89.

U.G.C., Annual Report for the year 1990-91.

U.G.C., *Annual Report*, 1974-75.

U.G.C., *Annual Report*, 1974-75.

U.G.C., *Bulletin of Higher Education*, Vol. I, No.1, April 1975.

U.G.C., *Bulletin of Higher Education*, Vol. 5. No. 1-2, September, 1980.

U.G.C., Report for the year, 1981-82.

U.G.C., *Report of University Grants Commission*, 1981-82.

Ulliah, R., *History of Educational Thought.*

USSR, 1973, 'Science', N. P. Agency.

V-20, *Encyclopaedia Britanica*, 1979.

V-Vi, *Encyclopaedia of the Social Sciences.*

Wonchoo, H. N., *Studies in Indian Education.*